DOWN TO
BUSINESS

IAN CLAYTON

Son of Thunder Publications

Published by Son of Thunder Publications
www.sonofthunderpublications.org

Each chapter in this book is an edited and updated transcript taken from messages given by Ian Clayton at different times over several years. There are some minor differences from the audio messages.

Cover art hand painted © 2019 Derina Lucas, www.derinalucasdesigns.com
Cover design © 2019 Gabrial Heath
Book Layout ©2017 BookDesignTemplates.com, with additional elements by Rachel L. Hall.

Down to Business / Ian Clayton. —1st ed.

978-1-911251-06-4 *Down to Business – Limited Edition* hardback
978-1-911251-05-7 *Down to Business* paperback
978-1-911251-07-1 *Down to Business* e-book

Printed in the United Kingdom, USA, and New Zealand

For Worldwide Distribution

CONTENTS

ACKNOWLEDGEMENTS

Collaborating with Ian Clayton to write this business volume of his revelatory teaching and personal experience has been an honour and a privilege. Thank You, Yeshua HaMashiach, for Your direction and lead along the journey.

This book is a life changing account of heavenly wisdom grounded out in the practical and another ground breaking milestone for us as we learn to live our lives ever more through the veil, in the ascended place. Our greatest pleasure in seeing Ian Clayton's work published is being able to unlock the experience of this reality for those wanting to find it.

I particularly want to honour the support, friendship and dedication of my two closest friends Mary Lynn Bushong and Sheila Bunch, whose company and assistance has made greater leaps forward possible than I ever imagined. It is so wonderful to be walking alongside them and the many other global community members whose help has been invaluable. There are too many to name, but just to mention a few: Sue Town, John Graham, Gil and Adena Hodges, Steve and Pam VandenBulck, Barbara Krueger, Tish Narh, Kim Stephens, Donna Cruickshank, beloved Melissa, Tina, Michael, Sandra, Rose Marie, Rebecca and many more, including proofreaders, prayer warriors and friends of wise counsel, without whom this book would still be a vision.

I also want to give honour and thanks to the many leaders and teachers whose support and advice has been so empowering, including Nancy Coen, Marios Ellinas, Matthew and Pearl Nagy, Liz Wright, Dr. Sharon Stone and others I cannot name.

We would like to express our gratitude and love to the many bookshop and distribution partners tracking alongside us, including Pastor Robyn Peebles and Sarah Tanumi in Australia,

Sharon and Brydon Nisbet in New Zealand, Elizabeth Gomes in Canada and many others in the USA.

We extend our thanks for the graphic design expertise of several talented team members, especially Gabrial Heath of Aspect Reference Design, who created the cover for us, Derina Lucas who hand painted the fine art used for the cover and Iain Gutteridge who helps us solve lots of graphic needs.

Our special thanks go to Rachel Hall whose help in editing and formatting this book was a pivotal support.

Finally, we want to express our affection and gratitude to Ian Clayton for his wisdom, encouragement and oversight of this labour of love, and to his wife, family and other team members for their support along the way.

Revelation Partners
Son of Thunder Publications
United Kingdom

WHAT OTHERS ARE SAYING ABOUT IAN CLAYTON & DOWN TO BUSINESS

Ian Clayton is a friend, a colleague, and a kindred spirit, especially when related to business. Over the years we have discussed and unpacked so many different aspects about how we believe YHVH wants us to engage with this part of our lives. Not as a theoretical process, but one that is practical, and based on real results. Yahweh's Financial Kingdom does not follow the world's financial models or its laws. It is shrouded in Mystery, and yet profoundly reliable. The Foundational Basis for this is an engaged, proactive relationship with YHVH and His Heavenly Realms as They relate to our lives and our businesses. Ian explains all of this in a way that is refreshingly unique, and in my experience one that produces significantly impressive results. I endorse his work here without reservation.

Dale Beasse
President/CEO, Bekerman Properties, Inc.
Toronto, Ontario, Canada

I have traveled to over 130 nations, and I have never met anyone who is as profound a revelator as Ian Clayton. His comprehension of and experiences in the realms of heaven far outweighs any other person I know. I can guarantee that this book on business will rock your world. It will become an essential reference for anyone interested in forming and/or leading a Christ-based business model. Your business mindset will be changed and re-arranged to bring you into accurate alignment with Kingdom business principles.

Nancy Coen
President, Global Ascension Network
globalascensionnetwork.net

People are fed up with religion – with information that does not work and with being forbidden to enter the invisible realms that are very much accessible to the sons. Ian Clayton is a true father of a movement in that he has helped the body mature and grow exponentially through his teaching and outstanding example of godly character.

The Body of Christ owes Ian a huge debt of gratitude for the countless flights worldwide, the love he continually releases to the Body, and his perseverance through much adversity and opposition.

Ian Clayton is increasingly being revealed on this earth. His teachings are impacting the globe, significantly. More importantly, Ian's revelation is being released within the framework of his depth of character, integrity, heavenly assignment, and the fortitude that has been developing inside of him. Ian does not only possess a mountain of influence: rather, an entire mountain range.

Marios Ellinas
Senior Leader, Valley Shore Assembly of God
Old Saybrook, Connecticut, USA

I wholeheartedly honor Ian for his excellence and consistency, and I encourage the sons of God to read this book!

We love Ian. His revelatory teachings clearly come straight from his relationship with the Father. He sits with Him and sees what He does and then Ian does that: just like Jesus taught. Ian's Godly advice on how to do business is the same. It comes straight from the Father out of relationship. It is the only way we should be doing business: completely connected and in union with the Divine. We recommend this book highly to you all.

Matthew & Pearl Nagy
Glory Company
glory-company.com

FOREWORD

Ian Clayton has been seeing and engaging in the secrets of the Kingdom for decades. YHVH has been preparing Ian to continue to be a forerunner in many fields of revelation knowledge. The business arena is no exception, for Ian is already an experienced businessman.

Ian is my friend for whom I'm thankful. He is mysterious to some. However, I don't know of anyone who loves people more than Ian. He cares that people who are hungry will be fed the truths of the Kingdom. He has so challenged my thinking, and I'm forever grateful that he holds nothing back. Yahweh has smiled on us all who have the amazing opportunity to hear Ian in his anointing. Wow!

YHVH is jealous of the revelation He has given Ian within this book, and yet He has given Ian a generous heart to share with us these amazing kingdom business mysteries. I believe without the understanding of the mysteries being revealed to us from within these pages, it will be impossible to know how to operate the way YHVH desires. I am convinced that we who engage these truths are to implode Babylon's business model of control and slavery. This cannot happen without a Kingdom model of business that Ian speaks of, for it will bring freedom to us all. Be keenly aware to keep honor in your heart as you engage the treasures of the words you are about to witness.

I recommend with all of my heart the importance of engaging this book, *Down To Business*.

Let us all be about our Father's business.

Aaron Smith
Founder and Senior Minister for Gates of Zion
Mobile, Alabama, USA
Founder of OPe Technologies, est. 2012

CHAPTER 1

EMBRACING YOUR BUSINESS

It may surprise you that business should not be the primary interest of business people. Our primary interest should be the person of YHVH. Our spouse and families should be second and then provision for our family.

I think I am pretty spiritual. Yet, I realise there is a practical application for spirituality within my family home, within my businesses and within the circle of people that I meet. I am the same in church, as I am at work, as I am with my family, as I am when eating a meal out, as I am wherever I am because it is just my nature. I don't have to try to look spiritual so that people think I am godly.

The Word says this: *"And I will sanctify My great name, which has been profaned among the nations... and the nations shall know that I am the Lord"* (Ezekiel 36:23 NKJV). We do not need religious activity and seeming spirituality to be mature or to have the presence of YHVH. Living my daily life and impacting the community around me creates an environment for my spirituality to find foundational roots to be able to heal the broken hearted, to be able to bring deliverance to the captives and to be able to preach the acceptable year of the Lord. We must engage in Heaven and learn how to administrate it upon the earth. If we do not have a grounding in the world around us, particularly in relationship with people, that expression of the Kingdom cannot flow properly. Then all we are doing is performing religious behaviour, wanting to be seen to be spiritual, chasing spiritual experiences, going around and around in our own circle, lost somewhere in ethereal space. All we are doing is spiritual activity that has no grounding on the face of the earth to impact the realm that is around us.

Please do not try and create religious protocol from the teaching in this book or any of my materials. It is not about doing things or having a set of steps to achieve a goal. It is about developing a relationship with YHVH and those around Him that empower us to do things here. The issue is developing relationship with the presence of the Lord so we can be mandated by Him. We need to remember it is *"in earth, as it is in heaven..."* (Matthew 6:10 KJ2000). If we do not engage in love on earth, all we are doing is just getting fat on our spiritual experiences and enjoying being seen to be spiritual.

Embracing YHVH, Hugging Family

Our primary relationship is with YHVH himself. That same relational connection with the Holy Spirit must flow through to every area of our lives. This is very important to allow the realm of Heaven to invade all that you are a part of. I remember years ago when I was first trying to discover an intimate relationship with the presence of the Lord, I was busy praying when He said to me, "Ian, give me a hug."

I said, "Well, You are a spirit being, I am a human being, a physical being, so how do I do that?"

YHVH went through the process of teaching me what I do when I hug my wife and the process of how I do it. When I embrace my wife, my children and my family, there is a process that I have been able to clearly identify. Let's focus on my wife for a bit as it was with her that YHVH primarily set the foundation for the rest. When I hug her, I do not just hug her with my physical body by putting my arms around her. The same way that I would embrace her with my body, I would then engage with my soul and actually draw her into my heart and into the love I have for her. I would literally reach with my heart by faith and wrap her up into it. Then as a spirit being, in the same way I would physically hug her and I would wrap my spirit around her as well. Holding her as a spirit, soul, and body being, I would then draw her into the covering of my spirit, my soul, with my body wrapped around her. I do not just say to her, "Hi honey, nice to see you today." It is important for the future to engage purposefully and with intent and with your whole being. I do not just hug her with my physical body. When I hug my family, I embrace them exactly the same way. I embrace them with everything that I am. It takes practise to do this. Once you have established the neural pathway and you are able to engage it properly then it can expand to other areas. I always practice in 'Jerusalem' my family first. I spent many weeks learning the process. If you have never done it before, then start. I would also suggest if possible, that as a husband and wife, when you become intimate with one another, practise this process. It is where you get truly knit one to another.

When the Lord said to me, "Now, give me a hug," it was confusing at first, since He lives out there and is a spirit being. He also however lives in me. Through identifying the process with my family, I was able to transfer what I had learned into my relationship with YHVH. I had to learn to take my soul and my spirit, and turn them inwards towards His presence that dwells in me and wrap myself around Him, taking what I am on the outside and turning it inwards to embrace Him and His presence on the inside of me.

From the process of embracing my family members and embracing the presence of the Lord day in and day out, I found myself at the point where I was able to be away from my family and still keep in contact. This is because I now had them firmly grounded in my heart and mind and using my love for them to maintain a connection with them. I practiced before being away, by embracing them, by cultivating my love for them, by wondering about them and my thoughts of them were not far away from them. I have spent time cultivating intimacy and relationship with them. When I am away from them, I have the capacity to draw on the memory of those experiences. I had built this to a point of being able to have the capacity inside of me to engage with the image of them in my imagination from photos of them. I had spent time with their face inside my mind and looking at their photos. So, when I thought about them individually, I could actually see their faces in my recitative imagination. Then, from inside of me, by faith, I would begin to draw near to them in my heart and mind holding them the same way I had been practising. I would, by faith (remember this all starts with faith and then builds to reality), wrap them up in my heart. Because we are connected in the commonality of love, I would begin to feel what they were doing, where they were and what their behaviour was like. This developed over a number of years to the point where I begin to see specifically what was happening and what was going on around them at that moment.

I have many memories of seeing what my children were doing or what was happening with them. When I would ring, I would chat with them about it. This became what they phrased "Dad's weirdness". My family grew up knowing Dad was watching and he would know. From my perspective it was amazing and a tool that I carried into all aspects of my life, including business.

From Family Practise to Business Practise

Because I have practised with YHVH and I have practised with my family, I now have an increased capacity to practise with my working environment. I suggest that you do not try and do this with your work environment unless you have practised with the Lord and with your home environment first. We need to be walking before we try to run.

I realised that as a supernatural, spiritual being, I had the capacity to envelope and overshadow the whole of my working environment in exactly the same way.

Most of my staff are a bit nervous around me especially when I am away, because they know that I see things. They know I operate in something because when I go away, every-thing seems to alter, and when I come back, everything read-justs again. They notice the difference in the environment. I am the Managing Director of this company. When I get back from a trip, they are glad to see me because it is like, 'Dad' has come home. The more you become occupied with the things of YHVH in this realm of government and learn to administrate from this point, the things of YHVH and a greater level of your authority will be felt in your working environment. A new level of divine order will begin to manifest.

Paul did an amazing thing. Paul says, *"... I thank my God through Jesus Christ for you all..."*, but later on he says, *"... I long to see you..."* (Romans 1:8, 11 NKJV). Paul later says, *"For I indeed, as absent in body but present in spirit, have already judged (as though I were present) him who has so done this deed"* (1 Corinthians 5:3 NKJV). At the time he said this, he was physically hundreds of miles away from the church. Paul knew the principle of embracing the very things that he had brought to birth: bringing them under his government, he would actively watch over them, thinking about them and their needs, meditating on who they are and wanting to know what would be best for them.

Adam received a mandate to subdue and watch over creation. The mandate for you and me has never changed: it is still the same. We have to brood over and watch over our relationships with YHVH. We have to brood over and watch over our relationships with our families. We have to brood and watch over our relationships in our workplace. This is the same principle that has very far reaching consequences and responsibilities for the future.

YHVH has called us to be sons. This means that we are allowed to be spiritual. After all, YHVH is a Spirit. We have to display this somewhere, somehow. The display happens out in the physical world first. We do not want to be like a Pharisee or a Sadducee – the guys who found that man waylaid in the ditch, lying down, and just passed by him. The man sees the priests come and just pass by. The priests actually went over to the other side of the road and walked past him because he did not want to get involved. It was the Samaritan who came along who was a Gentile who helped the Jew in the ditch. The Gentile paid for his room and board, and he paid for his doctor's bills. We have got to be like him. When you see someone hurting, focus your spiritual passion in a practical, relational way and engage him down here on the earth. That is our job, to bring all our spirituality down to earth and say, "Here I am." If you do that, you will be amazed at what happens. It is for this purpose that YHVH and His Son draws us into rich spiritual experiences, so that we will walk out His heart relationally with people on the face of the earth. Love commands a response; when you love somebody, it creates loyalty, and brings divine government.

Family Covenant: A Cycle of Love

Due to being so busy, we set up a covenant in my family. I gave my children the right to come up to me and say, "Daddy, I need a tank full." No matter where I was or what I was doing (I did not care if I was speaking as a guest speaker to twenty-five thousand people), we had this understanding that I would hug them until they had had enough. When I was released by them I would then carry on with what I was doing. I would not care where I was, or who I was around, if they said, "Daddy, I need a tank full," they had the legal, legitimate right from their father to come and request that of me. I would give them my time and attention, and it changed everything.

I have a family unafraid of being affectionate. There is a genuine expression of love within our family, and because I travel so much, I gave my children the right to have input into how long I could be away for especially when they were younger. They could say, "Dad, we need you at home – please do not go for four weeks. I need you at home." I organised my time around their needs because I love my family. If I cannot do it in my family, I cannot do it in the family of YHVH, and I cannot show the world that there is a different way of running a family, and of taking full responsibility for my actions.

I made my family priority as a businessman so I would organise *dad's dates* with my children individually, even when they were older. From the age of two to about eleven, they had a dad's date with me once a week. I would spend an hour and a half with them no matter what was going on. That was their date, and I wrote it on a calendar. Every week they had a date with me, and it created a family environment. That is being family. I saw the pattern first in Heaven. You see, YHVH as a Father had a date with Adam. He would go and meet with him in the cool of the day (Genesis 3:8). It was a Dad's date. I saw it there, the Father did it with me, and I decided to do it in my family. It changed my family life completely.

It is the same with my wife. I have *wife dates* with my wife. If we do not have dates, gradually we get so busy we forget about the need to communicate, connect, and actually just be with one another. I spent six months at home (without traveling) recently and thoroughly enjoyed my life around my wife. We love one another's company because we have mutual respect, mutual love, and our needs are met in that love. I do not need anything outside of that, other than the presence of the Trinity.

Personal Restoration

Before I went through a process of restoration in my own life, I can remember sitting with a feeling of being alone. I was not actually lonely but alone, I could not figure it all out. My wife and I spent a lot of time communicating about this area, and trying to figure out what was going on in my life. There were things that the Father was doing deep inside my heart.

My wife looked at me at the end of one of these times and said, "Honey, you know something, no matter how much I give you, you will still want more. I cannot give you what you need. The only one who can do that is YHSVH." She said to me, "You need to turn to YHSVH to get what you need in your life. Then from that you can minister to me and then we will work this out together."

Those were words of wisdom for me right from the heart of the Holy Spirit. It is called mutual submission one to another. She said it all out of love. As I walked through the process of sorting out what was happening, I knew from that day forward I would never be lonely again. And I never have had that weird sense of aloneness again. My wife's words sat in my heart, inside of me, like an eternity ring. I was able to get in the face of the Father, and get what I needed so that I could give into my wife's life and never have to draw from her.

Narcissism

Putting yourself first is narcissism. Narcissism is self-idolatry. The Lord began to speak to me about narcissism in marriage; how a man requires his wife to give him something, because he loves himself so much, instead of loving her more than himself. You should not demand stuff, you should love her because love commands a response. In her response, she will love you, and you will love her. Your love commands a response. You will want to love on her more and do more for her, and she will want to do more for you. It forms a great cycle, creating an environment for abandoned expressions of love one to another. This is how we are supposed to live our lives as believers, not on the dunghill that we have been taught by the systems of man with massive expectations and demands that are mostly not right.

Greatness Via Servanthood

Perhaps number one among the many things we need to get to grips with is this: the greatest among you must be the servant of all (Matthew 23:11). How is any man trying to rule over your life serving you? Husbands, your wife may ask you this question, "When was the last time you died for me?" It is amazing how the old mechanism connected to a familiar spirit will sneak in and speak scripture in our ears to justify our ground. This spirit often repeats scripture out of context saying things like, *"Wives, submit to your own husbands"* (Ephesians 5:22 NKJV). As husbands we must remember that there is a little verse that goes before it which says, *"Husbands, love your wives, just as Christ also loved the church and gave Himself for her"* (Ephesians 5:25 NKJV). If you want your wife to submit to you, give her something to submit to. If you are controlling your wife, you are operating out of Jezebel's court. Wives, if you are manipulating your husband, you are operating out of Jezebel's court. This familiar spirit has used this scripture to dominate, manipulate and create an environment that has made men believe that they have the right to demand things of their wives when in fact scripture directs us to *"[Submit] to one another in the fear of God"* (Ephesians 5:21 NKJV). It is about mutual respect and love for one another. The husband dying for his wife gives her equity, which in turn enables her to operate within equality. He recognises that she is on the same standing as he is, a son first of all before Christ. I do not mean a gender here but one who stands in maturity at the highest level. She becomes your equal.

Relationships First, Business Second

"When a man has taken a new wife, he shall not go out to war or be charged with any business; he shall be free at home one year, and bring happiness to his wife whom he has taken." (Deuteronomy 24:5 NKJV)

Before I was married, I trained as a grocery supermarket manager. I completed my training by the age of eighteen and a half. I had done in six months what normally takes three years. After I finished my training, I was put in charge of managing a supermarket that turned over forty-six million dollars a year. It had about a hundred and seventy staff. I was only eighteen and a half years of age. So when the Father got hold of me, I was already able to do some things.

That is what I was doing when I was first born again: I was in charge of a supermarket, working seventy-five hours a week in five days. All that was left at the end of the week was for me to go home and sleep all weekend. Then I got married.

The Word says that newlyweds should take a break from some of those things. That is so you spend a year cultivating a relationship with your spouse, you learn how to communicate, and those kinds of things. I was busy praying one morning, and the Lord said to me, "Get out of your work, find another job."

I said, "Yes, Lord," but carried on doing my current job.

Then a while later He came again to me and said, "Ian, get out of your job."

I said, "Yes Lord," but I did not know what to do. I was a brand-new Christian trying to figure out who this voice was.

I woke up one morning, and as I was busy praying, the Lord said to me, "Today you are going to get fired."

I said, "Yes, Lord." But I could not see how it would happen. I had a successful supermarket making about eighteen and a half million dollars profit in a year. It was not my business, it was a business for a big company in New Zealand. I was earning about twenty-five thousand a year in salary. A good salary all those years ago.

I went to work that day and the area supervisor was there with the director of the company. I had become successful partly because I was a little bit rebellious and I did not do what they did. I did what the Holy Spirit told me to do. I did things differently, and was very successful.

They did not like that because it was not their system. We'd had a night fill the night before they came around. The shop was fantastic except for one thing. In those days, you had to put a little sticker on the front face, right hand side of every item. My night-filler had stamped almost nine hundred packets of jelly and had filled the shelves with them.

I got fired because she stamped the top and not the front, so the prices were not visible in the stack. I could have lodged a complaint against them, but I knew YHVH had spoken. So I did nothing.

The Lord said to me, "The reason you have been fired is because you are killing your marriage at its very start." When you are a married business person, your marriage must be a primary focus. You must make time, prioritise and organise your schedule. The Lord helped me learn that in a very specific way.

My wife and I set out a plan to go away twice a year and have a weekend without the kids. My wife would go away and I looked after the kids so she could have some time away from them. At other times, I would go away for a weekend and do what I wanted to do. Now, I am away for weeks at a time (it gives her a good break from me, ha ha!). You need to schedule, you need to keep communication and connection with your family as a priority, and most important, you must maintain your connection with YHVH. It is vitally important to keep a connection, a live, vibrant relationship with Him. Do not become so religious that you miss that.

Some Saturdays I have to make time together with my wife after a very busy week. So, there are times I will not go and engage with YHVH in the morning because I want to spend the time together with my wife communicating. It would not be a very good relationship if the only thing I said to my wife was, "Hi Honey, it is great to see you today," and then I am gone. Then I come home and say, "Hi Honey, good to see you. Goodnight." You cannot develop a deep relationship with anyone like that. But many of us, when we get involved in business, treat our families like that, and we treat YHVH the same way. "Hi, Lord! I am too busy today, I have got too much on my schedule." We need to change our schedules if we have too much on them. If we have too much on them, we are not prioritising correctly.

Business Principles Match Home Principles

I apply the same principles at work that I do at home. It is me being me. My business is in the secular arena. When I show up at work, as I said before, my staff reacts like, "Dad's back!" – not just the boss. I engage actively and bring them under the umbrella of the government of Heaven. Being accessible and communicating are the key to building good relationships. I always communicate with my staff by asking things and developing personal relationships but with correct protocol. While at work, an example of taking a personal interest in them might be asking, "How are you doing? How is your mum doing?" This is also being spiritual, operating in the realm of the Kingdom. The Kingdom manifests through me and empowers people to come under the shadow of the covering. The covering of the umbrella of the government of Heaven makes them feel secure enough to express themselves and be who they are.

This takes a touch of humility. Do not go and be a spiritual freak. I think I am about as spiritual as anyone on the face of the earth. But I try to apply my spirituality in a practical way. I do mundane things like building cars because I enjoy it and I am allowed to do it. I do not spend all my time going around speaking in tongues week after week, going nowhere, getting too "spiritually" fat and lazy to do the work of the community.

Several years ago I took over the management of a swimming pool facility. I had no idea what the plans of YHVH were, but I knew He was in it, so I got quite involved in the company. In fact, because I could do so much, I got involved in a lot of things they did not have time to do. I seemed to have lots of time to complete everything. I would spend two or three days a week away from work, come back, and everything would still be running smoothly. The owners could not figure it out. They said to me, "Whatever you touch seems to turn to gold." Then, their other facilities started earning money. I would just go, walk around, have a look, say a few things, walk out. They would say to me, "Every time you walk in here everything goes up."

When they put me in as manager of this facility, the turnover went up twenty-five percent. I would expect it to happen. I embraced the atmosphere and the environment of my work, as well as its location. Inside the location and atmosphere were all my staff. I was not the owner of it, but because I was the high priest of it, because there was no one else in that role, I had a mandated right in YHSVH to speak into it, to decree into it, to govern and to influence it and to do everything I could to make the owners look better.

I did not do it for eye-service: I did it because I wanted to serve YHVH in the middle of the business. This is the key. As I was busy enfolding the business, it started to increase and everybody got happier and things started going well.

Years before this the Lord told me, *"When the heathen come to you, they will lay their riches at your feet, and this is how you will know it is of me, because they will say 'I want you to have it'"* (Isaiah 60:11 NKJV). Years ago YHVH told me this would happen. Now I am seeing the first fruits of it.

I make a conscious choice to serve another's vision to make them look better. When you serve another, you will come into the inheritance that YHVH has for you. When YHVH begins to use you in the arena of business, He will teach you about government. He will teach you about structure, because government and structure bring everything in chaos into divine order.

Kingdom Principles Learned and Taught through Business

I can remember a young man asking me, "Ian, what do I do with the money?" This is a guy who has his own home and he is a responsible man. Yet suddenly, I am being sought out for advise like his father. He asked, "Ian, what do I need to do?"

I was thinking, "I do not know what he needs to do! I am just learning myself."

I just started to talk not really thinking what I was saying and just blurted out to him, "Well, why don't you invest it?" I suddenly found I was giving advice to someone about something that I knew nothing about. With my thoughts reeling, I asked YHVH, "How?" He said to me that I was speaking in tongues in English. It was fascinating as I was also listening to myself speak, and learning a lot! I heard the Father say to me, "You need to get an investment portfolio that has many facets to it and you need to have a wide range of investments from currencies all the way through properties to shares." I was thinking, "Wow! Listen to that." When the young man left, I wrote some notes of wisdom for myself.

In another instance I was working alongside another young guy one day and he said the weirdest thing to me. He said, in a casual way, "You know Ian, I am really kind of thinking about my future. What do you think I should do?"

I just blurted out to him, "I think you should leave work. Go and get a managerial diploma. When I am finished here, I want you to take over for me." I found myself thinking, "My Lord, I am already programming and planning myself out." As a manager, that is what you are supposed to do, train others to re-place you. Being in management or owning your own company is no different than being a pastor of a church: train someone to replace you.

When you have grown as a tree before YHVH and you allow others to come under your branches, sit under your shadow, learn and get the blessing of your fruit from that tree, it be-comes a joy to serve. When you operate with the Father's heart and assume the government, all the wisdom that comes with the government will come to you when you need it at any given time. Because you are a spirit being, when you assume respon-sibility, you will begin to know things without having to learn them.

Freedom through Divine Order

Personally, I had laid all ministry down because all the doors of opportunity I went through before had all closed. At that point two years earlier, I laid the whole ministry down and walked into the business arena. YHVH had repositioned me in this arena for this two-year period to show me that spirituality is as important in business as the church or family. I had to learn to apply my spirituality in a practical way, in the secular world, and as a son. I so enjoyed it and was starting to succeed. I ap-plied everything I was learning about government, service, and authority from YHVH's world into my business world. At this point in my journey I decided I would put everything into the business, and then I could bless others. I could send and sup-port others, give them money, and they could do what they were called to do.

Over that two-year period I learned so much of what I teach today. Then out of the blue came an invitation to return to America and speak. This opened up the floodgates to invita-tions. I started thinking, "I do not have enough time now!"

Having learned how to apply practically the position of spir-itual government through overseeing and overshadowing the work environment (that started way back with my family time), I learned that I do not have to be present to know what is going on. From a practical standpoint, if I want to know what is going on, I could check the security cameras: but instead, I would actively embrace my business, look into the working environment and look into each of the different locations. Engaging with the learned pathways I had developed over the last ten years enabled me to do this. I would systematically walk throughout my business as a spirit being, observing what was happening. Here is the key. If you have walked this process out and learned how to operate as a spirit being you do not need to be there to see it, just as Paul did. This is just practising from the very beginning of embracing the presence of the Lord, from embracing family, etc. I allow my spirit man to see, and as I become familiar with the environment, I embrace it and make it my own as it also is Christ's. You start in Jerusalem, then in Samaria, then in the uttermost parts of the earth, the world or universe. *"...[Y]ou shall be witnesses to Me in Jerusalem, and in all Judea and Samaria, and to the end of the earth"* (Acts 1:8 NKJV).

I bring the government of YHVH and expect divine order to flow where there is chaos. Where things are wrong, divine order will manifest as we learn to pray from a place of rest within this area of government.

Learn One New Thing and Incorporate Variety

I have the objective to learn one new thing every day not only in the natural but also in the supernatural. If I go through my day and I have not had a revelatory download from the Holy Spirit, I will go and knock and find one. If there are places I have not been, I will go and find them because I want to learn one new thing every day. Doing that keeps my mind sharp. You get stuck in the doldrums of life doing the same thing, day after day.

To keep my staff fresh and motivated, I give them variety. I have a little clause in their contracts that says, "I will do any other work that is delegated to me from time to time by the Managing Director." I have noticed that YHVH is like this: He does not expect us to do the same thing all day, day after day. After all, He has the universe to explain to us. So bring variety into your environment.

The government of YHVH needs to come through our life in every area. It is the government over our family. It is the government in our relationship with our spouse. It is our government expressed in our own ministry, in business, in our dealing within Heaven.

I have learned to find the seat of the government of rest inside of me. I find that I do not stress about things any longer. If something is going wrong, I go inside of me to sit on that seat and on my mountain. I sit on the seat of rest, and I wait on Him. It is amazing: everything becomes lovely and peaceful. Nothing is too hard anymore.

Because joy is the fruit of a truly spiritual life, practically applied it releases you and your environment from stress. Sometimes people would ask me what is going on because I would seem to always be happy. I just say to them, "I am on the Holy Ghost juice." You see, the Father wants us to be supernatural beings in a natural environment revealing all He is. He wants us to be so supernatural that we are naturally super, supernatural beings.

YHVH wants us to function as sons in the arena of business. I did not even believe I was called into business at first. Now I realise it is all about YHVH's business. He gave me a business to teach me that it is more important to witness about Him out there than in the body amongst people who are supposed to already represent Him. YHVH will open up opportunities if you are willing to align yourself with His will, if you are willing to desire the purposes of the Lord for your life. Then, He will instruct you and show you.

I really love business and business people. I love being around them because they talk money. We have got to get to grips with money a little now to be ready for the next level. We need to get our focus out of the spirit of mammon and into the glory out of the supply of little paper notes and into where the gold is. I am looking forward to the day when we can cast a fishing line and a fish jumps out of the water with the flowing provision of the Father in its mouth. YHSVH modelled this for us:

> *"But so that we don't offend them, go to the lake and throw out your hook, and the first fish that rises up will have a coin in its mouth. It will be the exact amount you need to pay the temple tax for both of us."* (Matthew 17:27 TPT)

Opportunity and Lifestyle

I had the privilege of being able to sow into another person's life. A family in the church I was connected with at that stage, had been going through some financial difficulties. I was not aware of that, although I was aware that something was wrong. I had an appointment with the mother of the house. She said, "Ian, we have not eaten for a week." I said, "Oh, my Lord." This was somebody I knew! I said, "Listen, when you leave, I am going to give you two hundred dollars. I want you to have this as a blessing from me. I want you to buy some food for yourselves." Afterwards, she went to the supermarket with the ten twenty-dollar notes that I had given her in an envelope. She took forty dollars out, put the envelope back into her pocket, and spent the allotted money. When she got home, she took the envelope out, took the notes out and there was still two hundred dollars!

As we walk in the expectation of supernatural Kingdom provision, these things will increasingly happen. Whatever is in your life is going to run in those you give it to. If you are like me, I am looking forward to watching others take off and I am going to have to hold on to their coats and ride the winds of the move of the Spirit instead of trying to push it through. This is what the believer's life is supposed to be about.

Do not let your Christian life get boring or religious. Let's never institutionalise things or make the system an idol. Make YHSVH Lord and King and align yourself with Him. This is the key when you want to get down to business: first, embrace Him. Then embrace yourself, your family and others. This will allow you to reach out into our universe.

CHAPTER 2

MOVING WITHIN YOUR MOUNTAIN

A number of years ago, the Lord began to speak to me about me being a mountain – a house, the dwelling place of YHVH and the mandated governmental seat of rest inside my life. As you read this with an open spirit, you will receive the word of impartation that comes through the anointing, but I also encourage you to do some study on it yourself.

In my journey, the Lord began to take me through a place I did not understand. I would be standing in my meanderings of the Word through the revelation of the scriptures that would come to me while washing dishes, driving my car, or mowing the lawns. I used to love doing this because I could engage my spirit man and not have to think about anything except just walking up and down into the realm of His Kingdom. One day, I finished mowing the lawns and I was transfixed for fifteen minutes, just standing staring into space. One of my staff came up to me and asked if I was alright. I turned to him, assured him I was fine, and then walked off. I was engaged in the realm of the Kingdom. It would have been funny to have been a fly on the wall after this, as my staff tried to figure me out.

You and I can be seen and have a visible form in the Kingdom spirit world as mountains. As a mountain, we symbolise and carry a mandate from the realm of Heaven to look like both the Kingdom of God and the mandate of the mountain of God. We are each known as the temple of the Lord. I am a mountain, and inside of me is the house of the Lord. He lives inside me, and inside my life I have the same rooms in me as those that are in the realm of the Kingdom of God – the realm where He lives upon His mountain. The mountain is His house. *"There are many rooms [places to live] in my Father's house..."* (John 14:2 EXB).

Everything that pertains to government operates inside the mountain. In the mountain of God, you have areas and rooms like the council chamber of war, other council chambers, dance floors, the banqueting room, the wine room and the list goes on. We need to get a hold of all these things. The key in that mountain is the treasury room of Heaven, which is presided over and supervised by Melchizedek who is its chancellor. He is known as the Chancellor of the Treasury Room of the Father.

> *"Although the Jewish priests received tithes, they all died—they were mortal. But Melchizedek lives on! It could even be said that Levi, the ancestor of every Jewish priest who received tithes, actually paid tithes to Melchizedek through Abraham. For although Levi was yet unborn, the seed from which Levi came was present in Abraham when he paid his tithe to Melchizedek."* (Hebrews 7:8–10 TPT)

The wine room is interesting. When you go into it, there are spiral stairs that go down to where the wine vats are. The rooms have the smell of old musky oak and wine, not with an alcoholic smell, more like grape juice – a good background smell. There are three massively big vats there that look like old wood. These are the souls for harvest, the working of unusual signs and wonders and the revisor of miracles. These are for this generation we are living in today. It is a place where you can go, drink and partake freely of the supply of these from within the mountain of YHVH. When you drink from the barrel of unusual signs and wonders, you will release signs and wonders. It is a key only, not a place to think you are the focus. The Bible says, *"Taste and see that the Lord is good"* (Psalm 34:8 NKJV). So, you taste, and go and see, and then you can testify that He is good!

From the other side of this chamber, it has the appearance of being fairly large with big vats that go on for eternity. Although the room looks that size, it actually extends out to where one side is a door. Lots of people have been in this room but have never gone through the door. Whenever I see a door in the realm of the Kingdom, I know there is an entry to something else and I want to go through it. I have had my fingers burned a few times because I have poked my nose into things that were beyond the arena of the responsibility I had been given and the mandate that YHVH had on my life. But that is okay, because now I have the mandate. I was inquisitive enough to go and get my fingers burned, and then I was given the portion.

On the left side of this room, there is a door that opens up to where there is row upon row of stored wine bottles. The wine bottles are the testimony of the manifestation of the pouring out of the glory of YHVH in and through the lives of every single believer who has ever been on the face of the earth. Their record is kept here. I have learned that when you want to know how another person's life was and what they functioned under, to go and get their wine bottle and taste their wine. To me, that is wine tasting at its optimum. The most important thing to remember is that the role is to build relationship, not to just keep on getting stuff.

You can get spiritually drunk on another person's wine record. This comes out from YHSVH's witness of the testimony of, in and through them on the face of the earth. We can now have access to a portion of it. When you drink their wine, the vibration of what they carried of YHVH's testimony can becomes yours, too, woven together to build His Kingdom. Many years ago when in the middle of learning about how to do this, I felt led to drink Enoch's wine. A great thing about this is that when you drink from the bottle and put it back, the bottle is still full – so everyone can come and drink. The only way you can taste and then see is by participating and taking something of the testimony of another's life. If you want to know what YHSVH was like, go and drink YHSVH's wine. Every day we can take communion like this.

Another layer of communion is that every time you take it, you are drinking the testimony of the record of the glory of YHVH that He poured out in His life. You can have a complete portion of that. This is what YHSVH said: *"...[D]o this in remembrance of Me"* (1 Corinthians 11:24 NKJV). He was not just saying do this in remembrance of Me dying – that is only one portion of communion. There are seven different layers you can take part in.

At the beginning of my journey some twenty years ago, I happened to be in the prayer room of a ministry when I was in another nation. We were talking with some people who had all started to have mystical experiences. They asked me to help them with ascending, to go into one of my favourite places and take them there with me. So I went with them into the wine room as this was one of my favourite places that YHVH had been taking me to at that time. While there they drank from many of the vats of wine and some who were there became very drunk in the spirit. Most of those who were there still remember that time and the fruit that has come from it in their own lives. To me it was amazing to be in this room in the Father's mountain and see other people there, in the spirit, in the Kingdom, all together doing different things. Some would watch and then participate, with everyone being able to see each other. It was a great corporate place of union with YHVH. To me, this is what the Kingdom is all about.

We are supposed to know about the whole of the Father's house and His mountain and understand the operation and function of the Father's government. We are supposed to participate with the power that distributes out of that realm of the Kingdom. YHVH has given us a mandate to actually become mature sons, and the only way to do this is to understand the operation of His house. When I sleep, I go and spend my whole night there.[1] My body sleeps, but my spirit and soul man go in and spend time in the mountain of YHVH with the chancellors, going inside the trophy rooms and the scroll room, the treasure chambers, and the different court rooms. There I learn from participation while being tutored by either the Seven Spirits of YHVH or the cloud of witnesses. All these places reside within the mountain of YHVH.

The scroll room of remembrance is an amazing place to be given access to during this maturing process. Everything the Father has ever done is recorded there. If I wanted to know something, then I would engage with the Spirit of Understanding and ask her to take me to the scroll room. The things you are engaging with will be sticking out from the shelves that have the appearance of scrolls. When you are given access to this arena and you receive a scroll and unroll it, the words come off the scroll like a cloud and surround you. Each letter comes off and becomes a doorway of knowledge to what the Father did. This includes what He did before creation. You will see it, not just hear it, so you can have even clearer understanding and be able to walk in the depth of that knowledge. I want to stress here that this is not something you do as a petulant, demanding child wanting to get their own way. My introduction was after about ten years of learning, training, observation and being tutored to come to maturity.

---

[1] This is covered in a teaching called "The Night Watch," available on sonofthunder.org.

When I am in the Kingdom realm, in the chancellors' chamber, I spend a lot of time watching what the protocols are for the way things operate and what their functions are. With all that goes on there with the power of attorney, I watch what they do, what they sign, and the way they record things. All the decrees that YHVH speaks and releases on the face of the earth and out of His throne are there, along with the decrees of the courtrooms of Heaven. I so much want to be a part of it all. I do not just want to watch, I want to participate with it. You cannot participate though until you get mandated to do something in Heaven, and you cannot get mandated until you have watched, seen, learned the protocols, and been introduced by one of their company to that particular place of function.

People ask me about the ring I wear and question where I got it from. One of the chancellors who I had been tutored by came to me and told me I was going to receive a blue stone from the Father by the hand of a man, as a symbol of the right to be a chancellor of the court and to be able to rule over it. I went into another nation ministering there at a big conference. During that conference at the end of one of the sessions dealing with some bondages within the lives of people, a guy in the prayer line handed me a ball of cotton wool and told me that the Father had requested him to hand it to me. After ministering until the end of the meeting some two hours later, I went back to my hotel room with what was now a very soggy, wet cotton wool ball still in my hand, wondering what it was. When I was in my room I undid the wool ball and there was the blue stone in a ring that fitted perfectly onto my finger. It had been on my hand ever since, for some ten years, until YHVH asked me to trade it into the life of a brother in Canada, to let go the blessing of the past to be able to apprehend the blessing of the future. I had been given the very stone I was told about. It was one of the first physical manifestations that the Father gave me of this type. To this day I have no idea who the guy was. He walked up to me in a crowd of two and a half thousand people, handed me the ball of cotton wool and walked away. I have no idea whether he was an angel or a man, but I have my power of attorney.

Cleaning House

In some of my meanderings, I began to realise that with all the promises of provision which were coming from the Father, there were little things that would come and just weave in and out of my life that were not synchronised with Heaven and that would cause chaos. You can usually find demonic attachments or assignments around these types of things that are woven in and built out of a common desire that has nothing to do with what YHVH has planned for you.

> *"Catch us the foxes, the little foxes that spoil the vines, for our vines have tender grapes."* (Song of Solomon 2:15 NKJV)

I purposely go after those things by engaging them and going to court to deal with them persistently. I have recognised them as patterns of sin, iniquity and a vibration that is out of sync with the harmony of Heaven. Wherever there are inordinate desires or things that are wrong and do not fit in harmony with my usual relationship with YHVH, especially if there are little roots of iniquity in them, I go after them to deal with them until they are no longer there.

One of the key things we need to understand is that YHVH wants to give us the seats of government on the mountains. But until we clean house inside, we will never get those seats or the mountains. We must allow the presence of Holy Spirit to deal with this in our lives. We will never be able to come into the reality of possessing our inheritance in the Kingdom until we do.

In the same way that an individual is given a seat on a mountain to govern the mountain and all that pertains to its function, an ecclesia has the capacity to occupy one as well and do the same thing. A family, a business, a city, a region, et cetera – the list goes on. Through relationship with YHVH and the training to bring you to maturity, you must discover what the mountain and its seat is, so that YHVH can teach you how to handle it properly. Through maturity and responsibility, learn what it is to sit on the seat of government of that mountain out of rest. Allow His government in your life to move over the mountain and begin to influence the arena you are now responsible for. Do not just assume that because you want it, you can have it. This has the capacity to destroy as much as build life. Once the seat has been occupied and you have walked through what is needed to govern properly (this does not take a day, it takes years), you will then be given the capacity to engage that mountain and bring its government to bear. When you are functioning with it out of a place of maturity, you will begin to have victory in some of these areas of function and occupation. The key scripture is from Luke 19:13 – to occupy till He comes. Your name is then written on the seat and into the mountain that it governs.

I am not talking about your name being written in the Lamb's book of life here. I am talking about a recognisable and functional part of your role now in Heaven. The new name we receive as a son through YHSVH will give us access into heavenly places. This is about you coming to maturity and learning your function.

Galaxies

I want you to try and get a grid of how big you and I really are. As was so aptly said in a movie, "Awesome cosmic power, itty bitty living space." I am doing this to try and shift some of the small thinking arenas out and away from this frail human form into what our actual reality is and into what our perspective should be. I want you to see the dimensions of what you look like when we are functioning within creation. If you stand in the celestial arena as who you are in Christ and look at a galaxy, its appearance from the way we usually judge size seems to be so big. But because of the way we have learned, there is a hidden reality that is not yet fully perceived by us. This must change. If we position ourselves in the centre of a galaxy, within the image of who we are in the Father, scripture says He has *"... measured heaven with a span"* (Isaiah 40:12 NKJV) and *"... created man in His own image..."* (Genesis 1:27 NKJV). He holds us in the span of His hand. When we function as we are supposed to out of union with Him as maturing sons bearing His image and likeness as well as His size, how big we really are in this celestial and cosmic arena.

I have purposefully used my imagination over many years in that arena as an anchor for my soul to get to grips with the reality of my spirit being's size. I would practice through faith until my reality was sitting in the middle of it. You do not have to do anything but just stand there. I was amazed at how suddenly everything there began to take notice of my presence and looked at me with interest. In some of my experiences, I heard the galaxies talk about how long they had waited for someone to come. They said it had taken thousands of years for me to finally turn up. They looked at me in amazement as they saw me full of light, thunder and lightning, just as YHVH had created me. It is weird and amazing to think all this started from me sitting on the seat of rest, moving to occupy my mountains and then discovering the depth of what YHVH has in store for us. The secret is not to get stuck on an experience and build an altar to it, but to keep moving forward. My advice is do not get stuck in the birthing chamber of experiences but rather pursue maturity beyond them.

I am amazed at how big we are when we see ourselves from within His perspective. YHVH is so incredibly interested in us becoming who we are in Him.

In the middle of most galaxies there is a black hole. In my opinion, that black hole is waiting for us to come and let our light shine again and possess it to take charge of who and what was there in the first place. There are thrones that have been long unused in the galaxies of our universe. The galaxies of the bubble we live in are crying out for us to come and take our place once again. Again, this does not take a day. It took years of learning and practice, recalibrating my brain and soul to handle the responsibility of this.

YHVH has given us a mandate to possess all that He has made. He made it for one reason – for us to display His glory. Even though we have the capacity, we have still not grasped how big we really are. We can stand in the middle of a galaxy and orchestrate the galaxy spirals as they sing and worship the presence of YHVH. That is their one objective. Once we start going into some of these arenas, we will realise how much the adversary has kept hidden from us: he has made us look so small. We must understand who we are and what our destiny really is. Many of us think our destiny is to try and live a life on earth in the hope that YHSVH will come and sky-bus us out of here. Then we think there will be no more troubles in our lives ever again. For many people, that is about the full extent of their beliefs. The adversary wants us to focus so hard on the little things that we do not see and become the big picture. Sorcerers went into these galaxies and left their marks. They shut down and occupied the bubble that is in the middle of them, filling it with demons and darkness. Now these galaxies are waiting for us to come to occupy and orchestrate them.

The first time I experienced a galaxy, it was one that could be seen from the Hubble space telescope. The whole galaxy appeared to me from the side like a dinner plate. When I was in the middle, it looked to be about the size of a conference hall. That is how big it was in proportion to where I was standing. All the stars looked at me when I turned up, and they spoke to me and said they had waited with expectation to ask what I wanted them to do. This is because they had lost the direction YHVH had given them at the beginning.

"You are the only [alone are the] Lord. You made the heavens [sky], even the highest [heavens of the] heavens, with all the

stars [their hosts]. You made the earth and everything on it, the seas and everything in them; You give life to everything. The heavenly army [host] worships you." (Nehemiah 9:6 EXB)

"They fought from heaven; the stars in their courses fought against Sisera." (Judges 5:20 KJ2000)

"God set them in the firmament of the heavens to give light on the earth, and to rule over the day and over the night..." (Genesis 1:17–18 NKJV)

I am teaching this so if you have an ear, you will hear. I have had people who have listened to some of my messages ten times, and then ten years later they will suddenly get it. They will say they had never heard certain points even if they had listened to it twenty-five times. This happens because they did not have an ear to hear. When you do hear, it breaks the mould you have been accustomed to carrying.

As you possess your mountain and learn about its function, please do not hurry the process. Remember again this took me years, so it may well take you a similar amount of time. A baby does not become an adult in a day, and you will not mature in a day either. Enjoy the journey YHVH has you on.

CHAPTER 3

TREASURY ROOM INSIDE YOUR MOUNTAIN

Melchizedek is the Chief Chancellor of the Treasury Room of Heaven, and YHSVH is forever after the order of Melchizedek. *"...[T]he forerunner has entered for us, even Jesus, having become High Priest forever according to the order of Melchizedek"* (Hebrews 6:20 NKJV). YHSVH is our priest who resembles Melchizedek in so many ways; He is someone who has become a priest, not because of some requirement about human lineage, but because of the power of an endless life. Remember, the psalmist says, *"You are a priest forever—in the honoured order of Melchizedek"* (Hebrews 7:17 VOICE).

I need to reiterate that YHSVH is not Melchizedek, but follows the order of the priesthood of Melchizedek, who also has an endless life. I have met them both personally.

YHSVH is the chief trader in Heaven for all of humanity, who can take all that we have and all that we are and trades with His blood and body for you and me, to redeem us out of corruption. That is why He makes intercession for us continually before the face of YHVH: He mediates and He trades for us through what He has done.

We need to truly understand what YHSVH has done. It is amazing to me, that He would make a conscious choice to come into creation and make the greatest trade with His body in all its forms, to redeem us. The Bible says, "... *Jesus... for the joy [of obtaining the prize] that was set before Him, endured the cross, despising and ignoring the shame, and is now seated at the right hand of the throne of God"* (Hebrews 12:2 AMP).

I now understand joy as the liberty I come into when I hear the truth of what He did for me and the pathway He made for me, back to full restoration. I cannot help but proclaim how much I value, love and appreciate Him for what He has done, including the pleasure He has, in giving us the kingdom.

One of His greatest desires is to fill the treasury room of our own mountain. To become a pattern of heaven and to be able to distribute what He bestows upon us

I am very aware that YHVH wants to put the wealth of the nations into the hands of the beloved. I am not talking about a prosperity doctrine. I am talking about wealth transference, where a trillion dollars can come into our hands in a single day. The biggest question that needs to be asked is, "Can we handle that?" Do we have the capacity to handle it? Transference is going to start happening I believe, very soon. It will not just come to us because we call ourselves Christians, it will only come to a seat of government that is operating in His world already. It will come to that position on a mountain of government not to a person, but for the sole purpose of being able to bring divine order in the middle of chaos. We need to be able to distribute what the Lord gives us through justice and out of peace, not to appease any injustice that is prevalent in the world.

One of our biggest problems and issues is what the Word calls "the love of money". It can be described as always wanting more when our needs are taken care of. I can remember reading a book where a question was posed to a person. One of the wealthiest people on the earth was asked, "When is enough, enough?" The answer was, "There is never enough!" Anyone who has not had this issue of the love of money dealt with thoroughly in their life, will be taken through a journey to deal with it that will bring a massive load of repentance. They will have to work through their life and deal with their own trading floors and mountains. One of the things that will eventually happen is that we will all be brought into a revelation of what it means to have to deal with Tobiah inside our own mountain.[2] If you have never gone through this, then you may have the same problem that I had, before YHSVH took me on my own journey.

I want to take you on part of my journey through this. It is important that we examine our own lives before we begin to mandate something around us. We first need to have our inner parts clean. For this to happen, we need to understand repentance. Repentance is not saying sorry, but is in fact a place of conscious turning towards the perfect state of awe, to see HVH. As we walk through this and present ourselves a living sacrifice in a place of repentance, the high priest YHSVH can examine our inner parts and make us clean.[3]

"Search me, O God, and know my heart; Try me, and know my anxieties; And see if there is any wicked way in me, And lead me in the way everlasting." (Psalm 139:23–24 NKJV)

---

[2] This relates to the biblical account in Nehemiah: "I came to Jerusalem and discovered the evil that Eliashib had done for Tobiah, in preparing a room for him in the courts of the house of God" (Nehemiah 13:7 NKJV).

[3] This information can be obtained in a teaching called "A Living Sacrifice" from our website, www.sonofthunder.org.

My Journey

The Dragon's Well

The Lord began to take me on an encounter journey through a realisation I had, that there was a hole in the centre of my mountain that I recognised as a well. I would go to the edge of this hole and wonder what it was. YHSVH told me it was the dragon's well. I thought maybe it was like a well in the natural, but instead of being dry and full of snakes and scorpions, there were dragons at the bottom of it. I can remember standing on the edge of the hole, engaging to align myself and sync with the Kingdom. When I went down into the hole, I needed to be ready to confront whatever I saw. With what appeared like flashing light coming out of me and the weapons of war that YHVH had given me, I jumped down into the well. I fully expected to enter chaos, but I landed on what looked like a glassy floor. At first look, it appeared that there was nothing down there. Then I saw a short distance away what looked like a shadow, this shadow then turned around and look at me. I recognised it as a dragon. In my heart, I began communicating with the Holy Spirit. I asked Him why it was there, and what I needed to do with it. He said to me that it was the dragon in the well of my own mountain, and that I had to destroy it. When I asked why it was here, He said it was in my heart, living in my mountain in the well of supply. I was shocked and horrified!

I came out of that dragon's well determined to find scriptural references to get some direction. I searched a concordance, and I found this scripture:

> *"I went out at night through the Valley Gate. I rode toward the Dragon Well and the Trash [Garbage; Refuse;Dung] Gate, inspecting the walls of Jerusalem that had been broken down and the gates that had been destroyed [devoured] by fire." (Nehemiah 2:13 EXB)*

It is interesting in scripture that Nehemiah went from the Valley Gate in the direction of the Dragon's Well. (Some translations say a Jackal's Well. It was actually not a Jackal's Well; it was a Dragon's Well. In the original Hebrew, it meant a dragon, a monster.) Whatever was in that well controlled all the water supply for Jerusalem. Its position gave it the control of the distribution of finances, wealth and supply, on a personal level as well as a corporate level. When I read that, I realised I had the same problem in my life. I needed to go into my own dragon's well in my mountain, and deal with the dragon inside my life.

So I went in again and found that I did have a dragon in that well and that I had to deal with. What I discovered when I destroyed it, was amazing. I can remember cutting the dragon's swollen belly open. Out of its belly came coins, silver, gold, money, scrolls, and oil that had been stored inside of it. All that plunder had been taken from its occupation in my mountain, that was supposed to have been for me and my inheritance and supply, but instead the dragon had it caged and locked up, ready to consume it and use it for itself.

Over the years I have learnt some key basic things to do every time you deal with a dragon, that you must do when you destroy it. Hide yourself in YHVH - remember, they cannot see into YHVH's realm. Come out of that realm and cut its sharply spiked tail off, cut off its legs, I always stick my blade into the underside of its jaws into the head as a final act [sorry if this is too graphic], then cut open its belly and take out the spoils that have now become mine. Please do not do this through mental assent to information but by being led by YHVH through a pattern. Because of my ignorance and assumption, the first dragon I slew nearly killed me when its tail struck my leg and gave me a blood clot all the way up my leg; this took a year of living in pain to break down and dissolve. Lastly, I always trade as a love gift all the spoils of war. I would rather have an increasing relationship with YHVH than have stuff, so I trade/exchange it for relationship.

Dragons are not interested in servants. Dragons are focused on kings. The servant does not mean anything to the dragon.

Nehemiah was servant to a king who later released him to go and rebuild Jerusalem. He went back into Jerusalem the same way he first went in – as a servant, but became the ruler who exercised authority as a king while there.

The Gates: A Journey Through the Book of Nehemiah

> *"...I went out by night through the Valley Gate to ...the Refuse Gate, and viewed the walls of Jerusalem which were broken down and its gates which were burned with fire. Then I went on to the Fountain Gate and to the King's Pool, but there was no room for the animal under me to pass. So I went up in the night by the valley, and viewed the wall; then I turned back and entered by the Valley Gate, and so returned.* (Nehemiah 2:13–15 NKJV)

> *"...Eliashib the high priest rose up with his brethren the priests and built the Sheep Gate."* (Nehemiah 3:1 NKJV)

There were a number of gates Nehemiah went to: the valley gate, dung gate, the king's pool or fountain gate, and in Nehemiah 3, he went to the sheep gate which is symbolic of commerce and trading – heavenly trading. This is a good gate to put in place first in your life as you begin to deal with the spirit of mammon that sits in your mountain.

The dung gate was the gate where all the pollutants could escape. In our lives, this gate must be cleared so all the junk can be excreted in the right manner. The last gate Nehemiah went to was the fountain gate or the king's pool. This gate was about authority and dominion. If there are issues around the commerce gate, dung gate, and the gate of the rulership of a king, and if they are not all functioning properly as a triune, threefold cord, then you will not be able to contain the wealth that YHVH wants to put in your life.

Facing Opposition from Within the Mountain

In my study of Nehemiah, I realised that Nehemiah was travelling under a double anointing. He had a servant's crown on, but it also interlocked with a crown of the king. He could switch from one crown to the other. He came with a mandate of the king for supplies, but he would put his servant crown on when he came into a perilous arena. He did not display his authority in a major way until near the end when he started taking governmental authority by becoming the one who restored Jerusalem at the king's mandate.

In Nehemiah 2, Sanballat and Tobiah hear of Nehemiah's plan to rebuild the wall of Jerusalem. They laugh in scorn and despise him, questioning his plan. When you begin to deal with the financial issues of the thing that sits inside your life, it will challenge you and laugh. It will use mocking taunts that can leave you questioning if you will survive, except by your own hands. I call these voices in our heads familiar spirits.[4]

> *"And I said to the king, 'If it pleases the king, and if your servant has found favour in your sight, I ask that you send me to Judah, to the city of my fathers' tombs, that I may rebuild it.'"* (Nehemiah 2:5 NKJV)

Nehemiah was still a servant, but he understood that he was a servant to the mandate of the Lord. He knew there was a bigger work that required his hands. The king therefore released him from his duties at court to enable him to do the work that YHVH had placed on his life.

> *"Then I went to the governors in the region beyond the River and gave them the king's letters. Now the king had sent captains of the army and horsemen with me. When Sanballat the Horonite and Tobiah the Ammonite official heard of it, they were deeply disturbed that a man had come to seek the well-being of the children of Israel."* (Nehemiah 2:9–10 NKJV)

---

[4] See *Realms of the Kingdom: Trading in the Heavens, Vol.2,* Chapter 3, "Familiar Spirits." Available on sonofthunder.org.

It is interesting Sanballat and Tobiah were there. Because they had control over the whole of Jerusalem, they were grieved that someone would come to help the house of YHVH by restoring it, because they liked the position. When Nehemiah came with letters from the king, Sanballat and Tobiah began to mock the very man YHVH had sent to do His work. Even though Nehemiah had letters from the king, they tried to stop him from completing the task. Can you see the problem here? These two men had a tie over the king because the king would not do anything about them. There was a false tri-unity: Sanballat, Tobiah and the king.

In Nehemiah chapter 4, Sanballat, a Jew, opposed the work YHVH gave Nehemiah. Some of the worst struggles we face are with those who are supposed to be the closest to us. The most destructive and demonic things that come out of the spirit world, often come from those who are around you and use them to get to you. The Bible says, *"The tongue is a fire, a world of iniquity. The tongue is so set among our members that it defiles the whole body, and sets on fire the course of nature; and it is set on fire by hell"* (James 3:6 NKJV). Our words can unleash inordinate circumstances that can create an environment to destroy another's life through controlling or destructive behaviours, which can be a type of witchcraft.

"...[W]hen Sanballat heard that we were rebuilding the wall... he was furious and very indignant, and mocked the Jews" (Nehemiah 4:1 NKJV). The moment you begin to build a desire to live from the realm of the Kingdom Spirit world, the things and systems you have previously been connected to can get angry. This will often come by mockery and deriding the very thing YHVH is asking us to do. This may cause great distress in your life because it comes from those close to you that you would expect to celebrate what YHVH is doing. Your finances may start drying up, just different circumstances always showing their hand. You can guarantee that you would find a type of Sanballat sitting there, mocking you. Remember, he

was supposed to be a close associate or friend of Nehemiah, but his actions were surprisingly opposite.

Nehemiah continues to examine the gates, rebuilding and putting them in place. As he comes back into Jerusalem, he starts to get angry because he sees the manifestation of the spirit of mammon in his own people.

> *"There were also those who said, 'We have borrowed money for the king's tax on our lands and vineyards. Yet now our flesh is as the flesh of our brethren, our children as their children; and indeed we are forcing our sons and our daughters to be slaves, and some of our daughters have been brought into slavery. It is not in our power to redeem them, for other men have our lands and vineyards.' And I became very angry when I heard their outcry and these words. After serious thought, I rebuked the nobles and rulers, and said to them, 'Each of you is exacting usury from his brother.' So I called a great assembly against them. And I said to them, 'According to our ability we have redeemed our Jewish brethren who were sold to the nations....'"* (Nehemiah 5:4–8 NKJV)

It takes maturity to consult within oneself and make right decisions. Nehemiah knew the seat of the government of rest in his mountain, and he accomplished great things because of it. He knew how to engage the presence of the Lord out of the mandate that YHVH had already given him. You can exhibit emotions of your soul, including anger and frustration, but there is a process for rightly dealing with that anger. The Bible does not condemn it. Instead it says, *"Be angry, and do not sin: do not let the sun go down on your wrath"* (Ephesians 4:26 NKJV).

We see Nehemiah go in and begin to speak with great influence to the people who were charging usury. Demons and corruption are the things that charge usury, within and over our lives and over those things we have served. They require payment from us, and service for our sin of aligning with the spirit of mammon. The dragon in your well does the same thing

I was in a meeting one day and was told that someone had $10,000.00 to give in one cheque into the offering. A man at the back of the room then started to manifest opposition, repeating aloud that he did not want to give a certain amount of money. He was a millionaire. The issue is not whether you have money or not: the issue is what is in your life has control over you. Do you serve it, or does it serve you? The character Gollum in Lord of the Rings is a good example of this type of schizophrenic practice in the lives of people. Gollum is destroyed by the desire for what he considered to be "Precious".

Let's return to Nehemiah:

> *"After serious thought, I rebuked the nobles and rulers, and said to them, 'Each of you is exacting usury from his brother... let us stop this usury! Restore now to them, even this day, their lands, their vineyards, their olive groves, and their houses...' Then I shook out the fold of my garment and said, 'So may YHVH shake out each man from his house, and from his property, who does not perform this promise.'"* (Nehemiah 5:7,10,11,13 NKJV)

Angered, Nehemiah tells them to deal with their issues and release the debt. It is amazing how slippery the spirit of mammon is. Although YHSVH has released us from its debt, when we start getting blessed by YHVH in our Christian life and He begins giving us an increase, it is amazing how we can feel about what we have. We often try to protect it and keep it, even though He is the one who has blessed us, and we can still find it hard to give. We face an opportunity to give in an offering, and we vacillate between giving one hundred dollars or five dollars. Then we find ourselves saying that we do not want to give too much. The question we should then be asking is, does it have you or do you have it? The very thing that speaks to you when you give your offering lets you know what is going on inside your mountain. Remember here I am talking about on Old Testament theology regarding tithing.

The Bible says,

> *"On that day they read from the Book of Moses in the hearing of the people, and in it was found written that no Ammonite or Moabite should ever come into the assembly of God, because*

they had not met the children of Israel with bread and water,
but hired Balaam against them." (Nehemiah 13:1–2 NKJV)

Just a point to note here, the Ammonites and Moabites hired
Balaam to curse the people of YHVH instead of giving them
what they needed, which was a word from YHVH. We need to
be careful not to act with the same spirit when we see others
being blessed; gossip is one of the most slanderous things
against people. Remember men are just as bad as women with
gossip.

"So it was, when they had heard the Law, that they sepa-
rated all the mixed multitude from Israel. Now before this,
Eliashib the priest, having authority over the storerooms of
the house of God, was allied with Tobiah" (Nehemiah 13:3–4
NKJV). Here we have the high priest over the house of YHVH
allied with Tobiah, who was the one that spoke out against it.
You have three people sitting there: Balaam, who they hired to
curse the Israelites; Eliashib the priest; and Tobiah. Again, a
false bench ruling in the absence of true authority. The key is,
the gate to prestige and honour is in the floor, the greater you
push yourself forward the less significant you become.

The Treasures

"And he had prepared for him a large room, where previously
they had stored the grain offerings, the frankincense, the arti-
cles, the tithes of grain, the new wine and oil, which were com-
manded to be given to the Levites and singers and gatekeepers,
and the offerings for the priests. But during all this I was not in
Jerusalem, for in the thirty-second year of Artaxerxes king of
Babylon I had returned to the king. Then after certain days I
obtained leave from the king." (Nehemiah 13:5–6 NKJV)

"Then brought all Judah the tithe of the corn, and the new wine
and the oil unto the treasuries." (Nehemiah 13:12 KJV)

The tithe, corn, wine, and oil are four key things that are very
trade-able and were being lived off by the person living in that
place in Jerusalem. They are the very things that we need freed
in our own lives. They were supposed to have been for all those

who ministered to YHVH and being about His service. Let's take a look at them and their impact around us.

Tithes

Tithes speak of the sacrifices you have made before the presence of YHVH. The service of your hands and your life which is your time. (Please remember this is an Old Testament theology in Old Testament times.) The sacrifices are a continual fragrance coming up before the Lord from inside your mountain and life, through your giving. The remembrances of them need to be stored and put into your treasury room. This sacrifice is a treasure in your storehouse and in your mountain designed to be a blessing for the future.

Corn

Corn speaks of the increase of the seed of YHVH's growth in your life. It represents the maturing of your life experiences with Him. If you are immature, you will not have corn to bring into the treasury room. He desires mature Sons who know how to keep things in the right order, bringing offerings of their maturity. Even in doing that, they can still lay it all down to serve another.

When the Bible talks about a corn seed or a seed, it speaks of sowing. A farmer plants a seed in the ground. He does not expect just one seed back, but expects increase in the seed planted. He expects three or four ears of corn with an average of fifty-six seeds per cob from the one seed planted. This is the kind of harvest he waits to receive back from one seed. Yet remember, our mountain treasury and trading floor cannot receive increase if we have not first cleaned it out.

For eight years I stood at the back of my church, praying. In those days, my job was to be the support for the senior leader at the front of the church, by serving the house with what I had to give. I knew my place was to open up the realm of the Kingdom so that the glory and the presence of the Lord would rest upon him in a greater way while he was ministering. (This is a key: if you are in a body, while there you serve that body.) There were times when I would stand at the back of the church, questioning what it was all about and how it all worked. At that time I was going through and learning a lot of these things in my own life, and feeling the joy and peace of YHVH. There would be times when I would see YHSVH come walking through the back wall of the building. I would look across and acknowledge that He was there. Often, He would just look at me. Sometimes He would nod His head, turn around and walk out. I had fantastic fellowship with Him while doing what I was supposed to be doing there at that time in the house. Because of the fulfillment coming from this participation, I knew I was doing it for the audience of One, and that made YHSVH very happy. I would willingly trade what I had experienced for relationship and union with Him.

Maturity is bringing the full ear of corn into that room where the full ear can be given to YHVH's glory – where it has nothing to do with you, except your service.

Wine

The new wine speaks of the joy of YHVH through the fruit of your life. So many Christians live as though they are sucking sour persimmons, thinking their Christian life is so hard and that everything is a struggle. It is only hard because joy is not a choice that is being made and they do not go where they are supposed to go. This is through the veil to find the joy. They try to do Christianity instead of being a Son. Just doing the process and the systems and working through tick boxes of I do's and I do not do's, has nothing to do with the new wine. New wine means the joy of life lived in fullness before the presence of YHVH. It means living in His presence today in its fullness. As I am there, I am here – living in joy. New wine can gladden the heart. He is not saying, "Go and get drunk." Rather, it is symbolic of something very important. *"The joy of the Lord is your strength"* (Nehemiah 8:10). The new wine is the joy of YHVH pouring out in your life in an inexhaustible, continuing, fulfilling, overflowing basis all day. The new wine being brought into the treasure chamber can then be poured out from the room inside your mountain over and around you and your environment. That room should be full, and has the potential to be full, if nothing else is in there using what you are storing that actually belongs to you.

Oil

The oil is the anointing that you carry out from being in the glory of YHVH, in His mandate and power. It is not about the gifts. Gifts are given so you can do the work of a believer. The oil is from your engagements with the realm of the Kingdom and your personal union with Him. It is not there to make you look good. The oil is there so that YHVH can put a match to it and cause you to burn brighter with a more intense heat. Remember that in scripture this oil flows continuously from two golden trees into the laver that then feeds the candlesticks of YHVH. (Zechariah 4:2-3) The oil speaks of an overabundance and a running flow to continually fill and cause the overflowing of the vial of oil. When it is like this, the oil will never run out. Unless there is oil inside your life to burn, you have nothing to light the fire with and nothing to trade with on the sea of glass. If something is living in your storehouse in your mountain, there will be no supply for you to be able to draw from for yourself or to distribute to others. I am looking forward to the day when speaking His name, fire would start burning in my hand. We are not always going to need a match to light a fire, it will come by a word. However, if we do not have oil in our life, we will never start the fire.

Intimacy Creates the Environment to Arc with Heaven

I enjoy arcing with YHVH and having His fire open up. When that arc happens, it is just as it was with Moses at the burning bush: the arc, the angels and cherubim sitting over it, with their wings a hand-spread or arm-span apart. The ark was not just called an ark. It functioned as an arc as well. To create an arc, two opposite poles or points of contact are needed, like a fluorescent light bulb or a welding arc. This creates a contact point with power flowing between them. This is done to create an arc of light between the two. His name was the power that created the arc between the two wings of the cherubim. The high priest went in and spoke the names of YHVH which would create and open an arc of light between the two wings of the cherubim. This would then open up the supernatural Kingdom world through which YHVH came and sat between the wings of the cherubim on the mercy seat. You and I are that arc on the earth today when we open up our connection with YHVH.

He said, *"I will put My laws in their mind and write them on their hearts"* (Hebrews 8:10 NKJV). YHSVH said, *"I am the bread of life"* (John 6:35 NKJV). He lives inside of us. He says, *"The authority that my Father has given to me... I have given you"* (Matthew 28:18,19). The rod of Aaron is inside us, the government of YHVH. The showbread, also called Manna; the supply of provision, the two tables of stone with the laws inscribed upon them to give me assurance, all create the environment for supply. The arc of the glory of YHVH over the top of us creates the access we need to see His supply flow. This fire-light arc is supposed to operate over our lives: revealing that YHVH is present. This creates an unrestricted gate of access to the government and realm of YHVH and will often appear as a burning white flame or a tongue of fire. *"...He makes His angels winds, and His servants a flame of fire"* (Hebrews 1:7 TLV).

YHVH wants us to understand who we are. If we do not understand the function of the arc, we will not create the environment for the manifestation of His glory over our life. We have two cherubim sitting over us, a copy of the blueprint of heaven. You are the tabernacle for YHVH's presence. Your body is the very arc; the actual dwelling place of the Holy Spirit. The unlocking of the chamber of our body is to reveal the presence of YHVH to the realm around you. The Bible actually calls it metamorphosis.

The Word says that the whole of creation is waiting for the revealing of the sons of YHVH. He wants us to realise that inside of us exists the fullness of this manifestation of His personhood. As He is there, He is here; and as we are there, so are we here. He will reveal this measure of his image in us in the days to come. To assist in this process, we must culture within ourselves a treasured place so we can be revealed as the sons of YHVH; the authority and mandate of YHVH sitting within and around us, the covenant of your union in Him being fully displayed in your body to reveal His glory. Do not desire the thing for itself, but rather desire the relational intimacy and union that creates the relational connection. This will releases His desire into our life to display us to the creation around us.

Divine Favour

As we continue with Nehemiah, we see that He was a cupbearer in the king's court, which meant he was a servant of the Father serving a king. A cup bearer always tasted the food and drink first in case it had been poisoned, and stood as a gate-keeper of the king's life. Nehemiah walked into the king's court one day very sad, and the king asked him, "Why is your face sad, since you are not sick? This is nothing but sorrow of heart." Nehemiah replied, *"...Why should my face not be sad, when the city, the place of my fathers' tombs, lies waste, and its gates are burned with fire?"* (Nehemiah 2:2–3 NKJV).

"And I said to the king, 'If it pleases the king, and if your ser-
vant has found favor in your sight, I ask that you send me to
Judah, to the city of my fathers' tombs, that I may rebuild it.'
Then the king said to me (the queen also sitting beside him),
'How long will your journey be? And when will you return?' So
it pleased the king to send me; and I set him a time. Further-
more I said to the king, 'If it pleases the king, let letters be given
to me for the governors of the region beyond the River, that
they must permit me to pass through till I come to Judah, and a
letter to Asaph the keeper of the king's forest, that he must give
me timber to make beams...' "(Nehemiah 2:5–8 NKJV).

Here is the cupbearer asking the king for something. This
gives a fascinating insight into the relationship of trust and
personal knowledge of one another. The king agrees and gives
Nehemiah what he needs. That is what I call divine favour coming out of service. YHSVH taught: *"Ask, and it will be given to*
you; seek, and you will find; knock, and it will be opened to
you" (Matthew 7:7 NKJV). I believe over the next few years
that the divine favour of YHVH is coming on the face of the
earth and He will begin to mandate the kings of the earth, the
sons who have a well full and clean, and a mountain treasure
chamber full and at the ready. We have been knocking. He will
open the door.

"...And a letter to Asaph the keeper of the king's forest, that he
must give me timber to make beams for the gates of the citadel
which pertains to the temple, for the city wall, and for the house
that I will occupy. And the king granted them to me according
to the good hand of my God upon me." (Nehemiah 2:8 NKJV)

The king also came under the influence of a man who had
found favour with YHVH, *"the good hand of God upon [him]"*.
The favour of YHVH is coming on believers today in areas
where the current kings of the earth have held to ransom the
riches and treasuries of our inheritance. In that day they will
come to our place, and the kings of the earth will lay their riches at our feet and say, 'Who is this God we see in you?'

Now let us look at the children of Israel. When they went
into Egypt, Egypt was suddenly blessed with gold and riches.
The king of Egypt used a form of exchange, he instigated the

use of a scarab beetle as currency, requiring the children of Israel to exchange gold and riches for the beetle. When the children of Israel left Egypt, all that gold and riches were given back to them and went with them out of Egypt. The Egyptian people were more than willing to give up all their treasures, jewels, gold and possessions. Favour will do this with us in our coming out of corruption and into the future YHVH has planned for us.

> *"Now the children of Israel had done according to the word of Moses, and they had asked from the Egyptians articles of silver, articles of gold, and clothing. And the Lord had given the people favour in the sight of the Egyptians, so that they granted them what they requested. Thus they plundered the Egyptians."* (Exodus 12:35-36 NKJV)

Most of us do not even believe that this can happen or is possible, because we live underneath the spirit of mammon that controls us, and because we often do not have the chambers and well of our mountain sorted. A transference of wealth is coming to the body of Christ. I believe this is going to happen in our lifetime. However if we are not ready for it, and are not prepared to carry it and be responsible for it, then we will not see its power manifested. Instead, others will carry it and we will only be the benefactors of it. I want to be a carrier. How about you?

First a Servant, Then a King

Let's come back to the issue with Tobiah in Nehemiah 13. Nehemiah goes away. He came as a servant of the king, investigated everything and set everything in place as a servant, set his heart to do something, then went back to the king. Nehemiah was then sent again by the king to carry out the full restoration. Not only is he mandated as a servant, but he is now empowered as a king to rule in Jerusalem. There is a key point in this for you and me in the realm of the spirit.

Nehemiah came as a servant, uncovered everything and then came back as a mandated son, a king in his own right. He was given power after he was given authority to go. YHSVH came on the face of the earth, and then went into the waters of baptism. The Father said of Him, *"This is My beloved Son, in whom I am well pleased"* (Matthew 3:17 NKJV). He was given power, then went to His mountain of transfiguration. Then the Father said of Him, *"This is My beloved Son, in whom I am well pleased. Hear Him"* (Matthew 17:5 NKJV). This is authority. It is the same for you and me. He progresses from an immature, *teknon* son who needs to be trained, to a *huios* son, a mature son, who has the capacity to carry the weight of the Kingdom and display it. YHVH is looking for maturity in His body. This is the maturity that means when one of His sons is speaking, He is speaking.

Zechariah tells the following:

> *"Then he showed me Joshua the high priest standing before the Angel of the Lord, and Satan standing at his right hand to oppose him. And the Lord said to Satan, 'The Lord rebuke you, Satan! The Lord who has chosen Jerusalem rebuke you! Is this not a brand plucked from the fire?' Now Joshua was clothed with filthy garments and was standing before the Angel. Then He answered and spoke to those who stood before Him, saying, 'Take away the filthy garments from him.' And to him He said, 'See, I have removed your iniquity from you, and I will clothe you with rich robes.' And I said, 'Let them put a clean turban on his head.' So they put a clean turban on his head, and they put the clothes on him. And the Angel of the Lord stood by."* (Zechariah 3:1-5 NKJV)

The greatest thing about the realm of the Kingdom is that no matter what I am like, I can go there and get clean. I do not have to get clean to go there. This is the greatest place of grace, and what grace is for. The Scripture says that Zechariah put a clean turban upon Joshua's head. It is described as an interlocking crown that has a servant and a king realm locked within it. YHVH desires to do the same for us.

As we are moving and growing within a position, coming to maturity for this transference of wealth to be able to take place, we must never get caught stagnating as a people. YHVH is looking for treasuries within mountains where He can put the abundance. There are businessmen and others today saying that they know YHVH is going to do this, but they also need to know that He is looking for trading floors and mountains that are clean. He is looking for mountains on which He can pour His oil as the dew of Hebron over the top of the mountain to release the abundance. I believe this will exceed the glory of the manifestation of the riches of Solomon. He is looking for mountains to rest upon. He wants to rest upon the tabernacles of His presence again in our day. YHVH is looking to pour out to the mature sons today what He had forerun with Solomon.

Multiplication Defeats Debt and Lack

One of the key things I have learned is to use the principle of multiplication. If YHVH gives you something, break, divide and sow it. Do not just put it into one place. When you break it, it becomes two, and those two become four, those four become eight, those eight become sixteen, those sixteen become thirty-two, those thirty-two become sixty-four, those sixty-four become one hundred and twenty-eight, those one hundred and twenty-eight become two hundred and fifty-six, those two hundred and fifty-six... It is an exponential increase. That is how you deal with the mountains of debt against your life. The same way YHSVH blessed and broke the bread then multiplied it to build his own mountain of supply.

When YHVH gives you bread, break it and multiply it against the debt, and allow His power to come on it. He did not see the need of the multitude, He saw what He would do, and as He broke it YHVH gave the increase. He saw the mountain that it would become. He divided what He had, and then the mountain of supply came down to meet His portion. Every time a person broke a piece of that bread, it increased and multiplied and more came, because the supply of Heaven was sitting over the top of it. The eyes of YHSVH were on the Father and the mountain of His supply, not on what was in His hand. YHVH is looking for kings who will give Him their mountain and allow Him to break it and multiply it. Our job is to present it in a worthy manner, prepared and ready.

He wants a clean mountain, prepared and ready. You can apply this principle to every single structure and sphere of life. If your mountain is not clean, how can YHVH bring His abundance into a mountain when its resources are used for its own expression, or being controlled by something else sitting in there? If the storehouse of your mountain is polluted by a spirit called Tobiah, who is living in the place that was supposed to be for the provision to supply, the daily needs for Levites and priests to minister in the house of the Lord are not met.

It is fascinating that Nehemiah's final act in Nehemiah 13 is to command that Tobiah be cast forth from that store chamber, that it be cleansed, sanctified and prepared; to then bring the new wine, corn and oil back into the storehouse so it can be filled again correctly, with the supply to be used in the right fashion. We have to do likewise, to deal with whatever has been sitting within the storehouse of our own mountain, the mountain of our own lives. We deal like Nehemiah did, with anything that is corrupt and has been feeding and nourishing itself on the supply meant for us and the realm we are responsible for.

Only then will YHVH be able to begin to release and bring the overflowing ready abundance of His Kingdom to the sons. This has nothing to do with gender, these are mature believers, male and female, who have walked through the process and are prepared.

CHAPTER 4

RICH MAN, WISE STEWARD, PERFECT SON

My own experience helps to illustrate the wisdom I want to share with you in this chapter, so we are going to look at the businesses my wife and I started up over a twenty year period.

The first was a gymnasium that cost me a lot in capital investment. That business just about failed due to some deeply rooted issues inside my life. The Father wanted to get hold of those issues, particularly with regard to provision.

This first business struggled. I wanted to be wealthy so that I could be financially released to serve the Kingdom. The problem with that way of thinking is that I was not being a wise steward. A wise steward realises that our source and supply do not come from what we do. It comes from what YHSVH has done. YHVH had to break me open in my first business. My wife and I went through a lot of struggle. Once we realised that financial resources were not going to come the way I had thought, I decided it was time I became a wise steward of what the Lord was giving us. In the end, He turned that whole thing around. We came out far better than we went into it.

Some time ago, after being with a New Zealand local council for sixteen years, I was laid off from a managerial position. When I was laid off, I got sixteen years' worth of back pay, pension credit, and everything else. Through that pay out, the Father enabled my wife and I to begin investing.

At long last, I did not have to go to work. I could spend twelve, fourteen, or fifteen hours a day praying, doing whatever I needed to do, or I could just go and have fun. I did not really know what to do with my time, other than to spend it praying. I sat down for six months and wrote most of the talks that my books have come from. I spent six months doing that and then my wife said to me, "Why don't you start up another business?"

There was nothing about the swimming pool business that I did not know, so I decided to start a pool business from scratch. Six years later, I sold it as a going concern and got a reasonable amount of money for it. Then I spent a number of years managing another position in the swimming pool industry.

I like to work my way up in a business, because that allows me to know what work is like for my staff. So I started at the bottom. I did not have an understanding of where the Lord was going to take me. Consequently, I started off as a shift manager. Then I became the client manager, then the operations manager, then the facility manager and finally I became the business owner.

When you are willing to serve others and make them look better, the Father will promote you. If that promotion does not come by the hand of man, it will come in the realm of the spirit from the Father, as scripture says it is YHVH that raises kings up and it is YHVH that tears them down (Daniel 2:21). Through this process, Holy Spirit began to give me some simple keys that were important for me as a businessman. I will unpack these through this chapter as we discuss the difference between just being rich, and being a wise steward.

The Responsibility of Wealth

A tremendous responsibility comes with the transference of the wealth of the world. To give you an idea, in the Forex exchange, in excess of four trillion dollars changes hands every day. Considering coming into even twenty percent of that gives you an idea of what could be available to the Kingdom on a daily basis.

The church has always struggled with money. People build systems around money that are akin to a form of worship. Churches typically need people to supply the money to run them, but what would happen if the church did not need the people's money anymore? Suddenly, a different governmental structure would be set in place. I will tell you this now prophetically. I have been down the timeline and I have seen it: the church structure we know today is not going to exist for much longer, because in reality it is caught in a time warp and it is not doing the job that it is supposed to do – to present the Kingdom. It is doing a good job, but it is not doing the best job. It is not doing what the Kingdom requires. This is to mature a body of sons who know how to function in the Father's realm. Almost every church and ministry I go into is still bound by the need for money. Money makes the world go round and of course the golden rule applies, "He who has the gold, rules". Because I have not seen the transference of wealth yet, I know the current move of the Spirit that is starting to happen with miracles, signs and wonders is not the end. These are primarily designed to function amongst unbelievers to show them that YHVH is real. Only when I see the transference of wealth, will I know that we are in the final stages of the reality of a Kingdom move.

There are many financial exchanges made in the world, but most are totally controlled by principalities and powers that are controlling the financial systems. Finances used to be based on, or tied to the value of gold. Though gold is just a by-product of the glory, where the gold is, there the glory is also. Whoever has the gold, rules: the demonic realm knows this. In order to prevent believers from getting their inheritance, a culture of poverty has pervaded the current system which makes most of us blind to the function of the necessity of wealth. The adversary has come in and taken as much of the gold as possible; through circumstances he has put it into storehouses in the form of organisations controlled and influenced by demonic spirits. The G7 is a group of seven highly industrialised nations (Canada, France, Germany, Italy, Japan, the UK, and the US) that coordinate economic policy in the earth, together with the G12, G13, G20 and the G70. All of these structures are influenced by principalities that govern and control the flow of finances.

For example, there is a scarcity of oil because the policy groups allow only so much oil to be produced. Through controlling production, they can manipulate the price of oil. An example of this is that there is enough oil in Alberta, Canada to supply the whole North American continent for years to come, but organisations manipulate what goes on around the world and stop this from happening. False government (rather than legitimate government) has held the mountains of influence they have built on wealth, through the spirit realm, and it has exerted pressure on the face of the earth to control and manipulate our environment and the way we think.

When you start talking about wealth, many corrupt influences get agitated and will listen, to in attempt to manipulate our environments to control the way we think about finances. They want to stop the sons of YHVH from coming into influence and being able to do what we are called to do. Nothing can stop what YHVH has planned except us and our responses to wealth, because it is written in scripture that we will inherit the substance of the wealth of the earth.

Golden Glory

The Bible says, *"The silver is Mine, and the gold is Mine..."* (Haggai 2:8 NKJV), and *"... The wealth of the sinner is stored up for the righteous"* (Proverbs 13:22 NKJV). It has always been about gold.

In the Valley of the Kings in Egypt, a tomb that archaeologists did not know existed was uncovered a number of years ago. The gold brought out of the tomb had been buried in the ground for thousands of years. In later generations, the Israelites knew whoever has the gold has the glory: the Temple itself was laced with gold.

I am introducing a principle: Where the gold is, there is the glory. Where the glory is, there is blessing. You can see this principle in action with Obed-Edom, a non-believer. He had the gold-covered Ark of God inside his house. *"The ark of the Lord remained in the house of Obed-Edom the Gittite three months. And the Lord blessed Obed-Edom and all his household"* (2 Samuel 6:11 NKJV). The glory was over the Ark. Imagine having the glory of God in your living room, day after day. It was the first TV screen. I do not know how Obed-Edom got sleep with the light in his house from that divine glory. The principle is the vessel carrying the glory-presence of the Lord was so precious that it was covered in gold, signifying to everyone, "The glory is here."

YHVH is beginning to unlock the doors that have been locked to believers for a long time, because we are starting to deal with the issues of financial growth and who we are in the Kingdom world: we have been designed and chosen to be those who are to govern over the face of the whole earth. It is all about the glory of the Lord filling the face of the earth again.

Has Money Got You or Have You Got Money?

I will ask this question: has money got you, or have you got it? If you do not rule over money with the right set of values, it will devour you. When you get money through living under the system of the world, you will always want more because you desire to live in a better system. I know people who earn two hundred and thirty-four million dollars a month, but they still want more money! There are many very poor people who would benefit from a small portion of the billions of dollars that change hands every day. Our responsibility is to take care of the earth and all that is in it. If people spend it just because they have it and are not wise stewards, then the money has got them. It will devour them and it will become their god.

The Bible says you cannot serve two masters. You serve either YHVH or mammon. Mammon is love of money. The devouring force behind selfish financial gain is the spirit of mammon. I describe mammon as a little, black, hairy, mongrel demon who wants you to serve it. It will devour your sustenance and your financial gain if you allow it to. It knows that you will always want more, so it will ensure you stay having just enough but not a ready overflowing abundance.

My wife and I have set a personal budget. We live within an extremely modest budget by almost anyone's standard, which includes all of our monthly expenses. The rest of the money that comes to us needs to serve another and be at the disposal of YHVH. It is not about you and me but about YHVH's plan for creation. If we handle the small we will be able to handle the big. This is wise stewardship.

I have friends who are billionaires. You would not know they were wealthy because they walk around in scruffy jeans and a t-shirt. I call these the *hidden ones*. They do not care about an inappropriate display of their wealth, because they know they are wise stewards. It does not belong to them; it is the Father's.

One friend has an amazing car. The outside of it is not amazing, but the inside is amazing. I love motor vehicles. This car has a twelve-cylinder motor in it, although the car itself is beat-up on the outside and rusty.

I asked my friend, "Why do you do this?"

He said, "Because people do not steal dirty cars, and I want a good engine."

This thing will drag off anything on the road. It will travel at about 300 miles an hour. My friend said, "Ian, I only own one car. I am living within the boundaries of the budget that I have set for myself. I have got one lovely pair of shoes, and I do not need any more, so I have sandals that I walk around in. I have got one suit, a very expensive Versace suit. I wear it when I need to go to weddings and official occasions, but other than that I wear t-shirts and jeans."

We do not need to serve the bondage of financial gain but rather make it serve YHVH through us. If you are a wise steward, the Lord sees you governing the small things, and He will give you more.

Personally, I have had to learn how to become a wise steward, and to hold everything with an open hand. The key is to remain as a steward, stewarding what YHVH has put into your hands. As Paul says,

> *"...I have learned to be satisfied in any circumstance. I know what it means to lack, and I know what it means to experience overwhelming abundance. For I'm trained in the secret of overcoming all things, whether in fullness or in hunger. And I find that the strength of Christ's explosive power infuses me to conquer every difficulty."* (Philippians 4:11–13 TPT)

> *"We may suffer,*
> *yet in every season we are always found rejoicing.*
> *We may be poor,*
> *yet we bestow great riches on many.*
> *We seem to have nothing,*
> *yet in reality we possess all things."* (2 Corinthians 6:10 TPT)

The attitude of a son stewarding his father's wealth needs to be cultivated inside you. This in turn will generate the atmosphere around you which becomes a magnet for the financial blessing that YHVH wants to bring upon the earth. This attitude has the capacity (like a noise, a song, and a vibration that together become a magnet), for the abundance of the earth to come to you. It is this inner attitude that the Lord wants us to cultivate within us. In many people's hearts there is a familiar spirit that continually talks to us demanding more and always saying, "You do not have enough for tomorrow."

I love doing things in communities where people have next to nothing and are on the base line of zero. When you give them something, they rejoice as they now have abundance above the zero-base line and think they have come way up above it. Whereas in the western world if you give someone a million dollars, it may only get them out of debt to zero-base or just above.

We have lotto in New Zealand, and people win three or four million dollar prizes. In a year, most winners spend that three or four million dollars and have nothing left, and many are now worse off because of it. The desire for more things devours their sustenance, because they do not do what is right with their money.

Are You a Rich Man or a Wise Steward?

Psalm 24:1 says, *"The earth is the Lord's, and all its fullness, The world and those who dwell therein"* (NKJV).

The greatest controversy in the world today is who shall rule, because the golden rule on the face of the earth is whoever has the gold, rules. All conflict comes down to the issue of who will rule, whose will prevails, and who will have the finances to make their will happen.

Scripture says, *"... I do not seek My own will but the will of the Father who sent Me"* (John 5:30 NKJV).

One of the key questions we need to answer is whose will do we want to serve? Do I want to be a rich man or a wise steward? If I am a wise steward, I will serve His will. If I am a rich man, I will serve my will. The difference is between being a steward and being the owner.

Here are some definitions. The word *owner* in the Bible is the Hebrew word *baal*.5 Amazing, yes? The owner is *baal*. Baal means a master, or one with dominion. It also means a husband with supreme authority – one in control.

By contrast, the word steward is the Greek word *oikonomeo*, which means a house manager, an overseer, a treasurer, or one who administers the property of another.6

When you are a wise steward, you recognise that the finances you have flowing through your hands, are not your property. It is the property of another. His title is King of kings and Lord of lords.

One of the biggest idols in Israel's day was the god Baal. If you are a rich man and you worship self with that wealth you are a baal. That is the definition of an owner in Hebrew: baal. No wonder we have trouble trying to encounter the presence of God! The Word says, "...*it is easier for a camel to go through the eye of a needle than for a rich man to enter the kingdom of God*" (Matthew 19:24 NKJV).

An owner has legal right of possession or the right to rule. The property or the finances belong to him. He has the final say. He calls all the stewards to account, and he can do with the goods as he wants. He delegates authority to others.

A steward has no legal rights beyond what the owner gives him. A steward holds a position of trust. He cares for the goods that belong to another. He makes decisions but does not have the final say. A steward must give account to the owner. In all circumstances he must consider the will and desires of the owner, and is under the authority of the owner.

The death of our physical bodies makes it very clear that we are stewards, and not owners of our own bodies. When you

---

5 See entry H1167 of James Strong, *The Exhaustive Concordance of the Bible*. Cincinnati: Jennings & Graham, 1890.

6 See entry G3621, *Ibid*.

own something, it is yours to give over to someone else. When you are a steward, it already belongs to someone else.

Ownership is the Lord's

There are three ways that anyone becomes an owner.

1) You make something;

2) You buy something; or,

3) You are given something.

YHVH is the legal owner of all things.

1) YHVH created the earth;

2) He bought it with His Son; and,

3) He gave it to you and me.

"All things were created through Him and for Him" (Colossians 1:6 NKJV).

YHSVH is the true owner of all the finances of the earth. YHSVH is the true owner of all the naturally occurring resources of the earth. YHSVH is the owner of all the oil. YHSVH is the owner of all the witty inventions that generate lots of money for people. YHSVH is the owner of the fullness of the earth. All the gold and the silver belong to Him. All the currencies belong to Him. He is not subject to the currencies, but the currencies of the earth are subject to Him.

YHSVH said this: *"All authority has been given to Me in heaven and on earth"* (Matthew 28:18 NKJV).

Stewardship is Given to Sons

YHVH has given you the stewardship of all that He owns. Adam was given a mandate at the very beginning: Go and subdue the earth. He gave it up. What did he give up? He gave up all the wealth and all the resources of the earth to the accuser.

YHSVH has come to bring those resources back to the house of the Lord again. This includes natural riches like oil and gas. We need to expand our vision from thousands of dollars to millions, to tens of millions, to billions. We need to start to think differently. If you have a hundred dollars and you live off a hundred dollars, then think thousands of dollars. If you have a thousand dollars and you live off a thousand dollars, then think hundreds of thousands. If you have hundreds of thousands, then think in millions. Always keep thinking bigger than your current circumstances. The key to inheritance is dreaming combined with reality.

"...God took the man, and put him into the garden of Eden to dress it and to keep it" (Genesis 2:15 KJV). The word *dress* here means to be a husbandman and to serve. The word *keep* means to hedge about, to guard, to keep, and to protect from an enemy. We have done a horrible job of protecting what the Lord gave us from the adversary. In fact, we have lost most of it to the adversary. That is why I am so excited about being connected with people who are going after the inheritance. It is wonderful to be around them. As I have said before, this acts like a magnet because the inheritance comes to those who desire it. *"Therefore I say unto you, What things soever ye desire, when ye pray, believe that ye receive them, and ye shall have them"* (Mark 11:24 KJV). This is not to become wealthy but to become a steward, a protector of your inheritance. This is also not a set of tick boxes to do to get rich. It is about the development of a cultured life of union with YHVH and being discipled into our future by YHVH himself.

As a steward, Adam was given responsibility to protect and to cultivate what was entrusted to him. As stewards of creation, we are supposed to be stewards of the vision that YHVH has designed for us within the scope of being a son. We are called to be responsible to protect, promote and participate in its function. All of us are stewards of what YHVH has entrusted us, starting at home and moving into creation.

"The Lord... has pleasure in the prosperity of His servant" (Psalm 35:27 NKJV). Many years ago, as I was coming through the process of maturity from a servant to a friend and son of YHVH, I used to wear an earring. This was part of a

process YHVH took me through on a personal level. I chose to become a bondservant by following the scriptural process.[7] Years later, YHVH took me through the birthing chamber of experience to bring me out of my slave-servant mentality to become a son, releasing me from being a bondservant to the process of maturing into sonship. The Father takes pleasure in our lives to prosper us, as we grow in responsibility in His world.

A Different Prosperity Doctrine

I do not believe in the prosperity doctrine. Well, I do... but I do not. I do not believe in the prosperity doctrine as it has been presented, that if you give me four hundred dollars of your money, you are going to be blessed with four hundred thousand dollars. I do believe if you give with an open hand, being motivated by YHVH and in demonstrate demonstration of your stewardship, then the Lord can bless you with increase – but not necessarily with four hundred thousand dollars. The key is your openness of heart, and your attitude in giving. If your motivation is to get, then you are already back in bondage.

I dislike excessively the emotional manipulation of people during conference offerings by those who are hosting a conference, of people during conference offerings. I also dislike the manipulation of people through messages that are guilt-driven messages and with have an underlying agenda. I have seen on a personal level, those who take offerings from people with all the promises in the world, but no fruit. I have witnessed the trading platforms of people who say things like "Send me a thousand dollars today and I will send you a bar of soap, and

---

[7] *"But if the servant plainly states, 'I love my master, my wife and my children, and I will not go out free,' then his master is to bring him to God, then take him to a door or to a doorpost. His master is to pierce his ear through with an awl, and he will serve him forever"* (Exodus 21:5-6 TLV).

when you wash with it you will be healed." This stuff really annoys me because they are manipulating a valid principle and the law of sowing and reaping.

I understand the principle of a memorial offering. When my wife and I were close to bankruptcy, we had only five thousand dollars' worth of equity left. The Lord spoke to us both about sowing this full amount at the point of our need. When I spoke to my wife, we agreed to do this. This was the key: YHVH speaking and revealing what He wanted us to do. So we emptied our bank accounts until we had nothing left. We gave five thousand dollars to the church. I did not care what the church did with it as we gave in direct response to what YHVH had asked us. Once given, it is the receiver's responsibility to do with it as YHVH instructs. Again this is a major key: when you give with an open hand, once it leaves your hands it ceases to be yours and becomes irrelevant to you other than YHVH's response. We gave it as a memorial offering. We held it up and said, "Lord, this is in remembrance of Your blessings and Your glory. No matter what happens, we are going to praise You and give You glory."

About eight months later, because of our response YHVH was able to clear our significant debts from a business failure. You must understand that the Lord does these things when we respond directly to Him. I do not mean to imply that it is going to happen instantly to you: this was our journey through Him teaching us. The unfolding of our memorial offering is still happening today. Above all, I want to be a steward. I want to see this wealth enable the sons and daughters of YHVH to stand up and be who they are. I want them to be a blessing to bring the glory of the Lord back into the face of the earth.

A Tree of Blessing

I want to be a tree of blessing within creation that is always fruitful and with a river that never runs dry. The Bible talks about Nebuchadnezzar as if he were a tree. It says that as a tree, he "*...could be seen to the ends of all the earth.... And all flesh was fed from it*" (Daniel 4:11,12 NKJV). Personally I want to be planted as a tree in creation, able to overshadow the earth in maturity, and to be able to precipitate what YHVH is wanting in creation. To be able to cause prospering in environments that have only known poverty, to enable the earth to come into divine order again. Hallelujah! YHSVH will be able to bring redemption and restoration.

> "*... He chose us in Him before the foundation of the world, that we should be holy and without blame before Him in love, having predestined us to adoption as sons by Jesus Christ to Himself, according to the good pleasure of His will, to the praise of the glory of His grace, by which He made us accepted in the Beloved. In Him we have redemption through His blood, the forgiveness of sins, according to the riches of His grace.*" (Ephesians 1:4–7 NKJV)

It is the Word of YHVH that redeems. *Redemption* in Ephesians 1 means to purchase at the market place, to ransom, to loose from bondage by paying a price, or to be the next of kin who buys back a relative's property lost by mismanagement.

We are going to be able to buy back assets from those who have mismanaged them with finances, as sons on the face of the earth. First, we have to get the attitude of our inner man sorted and change our heart's wrong motives and desires regarding finances, to what is right.

My business produces a good annual revenue. I take a salary out of that income. I could take more, but I choose to pay the extra to my staff and use it in better ways. Last year, I made a nice profit. So I am finding ways I can give that back to my staff who labour for me in the business. As long as I meet my budget for my basic living expenses and live within my means, that is all I am concerned about.

I want to be a blessing to others and show myself a steward of what YHVH gives me, whether it is much or little does not matter. I want .to become a tree planted like Solomon, so that others can come and dwell under the shade and the branches of that tree, and be blessed.

YHVH's mandate to Adam was for him to prosper and be fruitful, to multiply as a steward. This required him to nurture, to cultivate and to protect everything from the serpent. YHVH gave Adam great freedom as a steward, but also set boundaries that recognised the Lord as the owner. As a steward, you need to recognise the boundaries that YHVH sets as an owner.

A guy I know had been trading at a profit of forty percent per month with his investment portfolio, and he tried to go over the fifty percent barrier. He would trade one month at a good percentage above forty percent on his investment. But he found that he could not maintain it. He would go down to thirty-two percent, then thirty-five percent, thirty-six percent and then back to forty percent. He could not trade over forty percent. Another brother in conversation said to him, "Excuse me. Don't you think the Lord may have capped it at forty percent?" This was his boundary that YHVH had set. So he learned to steward the forty percent, instead of allowing the thing to eat into him to want sixty-five percent.

If you start off with a million dollars at the beginning of the month, and you can trade at one percent a day compounding, you end up with considerably more at the end of the month. To me, that is good multiplication!

When you learn how to handle what He is giving you as a steward and you steward it well, He may be able to release to you the thousand-fold return. With the Lord, the sky really is the limit, because He owns it all anyway. He wants to give back to us to become a blessing to others to make His name famous.

The Bible says, "*...all things come from You, And of Your own we have given You*" (1 Chronicles 29:14 NKJV). YHVH owns everything.

A good steward acknowledges the true owner. The Lord calls every steward to give an account. "*...Each of us shall give an account of himself to God*" (Romans 14:12 NKJV).

"...The lord of those servants came and settled accounts with them" (Matthew 25:19 NKJV).

Now here is the most amazing thing. If you are an owner and not a steward, in that day when YHVH calls you to account, if you have not done what He has asked you to do, He will call you a foolish servant. He will call you foolish and say, "Take it away from the foolish one and give it to him who has been a wise steward." So if you are just a rich man, you are going to lose the whole lot to someone who is a wise steward. To those who have been wise stewards, God says, *"You have done well, and proven yourself to be my loyal and trustworthy servant. Because you were faithful to manage a small sum, now I will put you in charge of much, much more"* (Matthew 25:23 TPT).

When you learn how to handle billions and trillions of dollars, it becomes a small thing to handle millions. Get this in your head: when you deal with the riches of Heaven, a trillion dollars is a small thing! It is nothing in comparison to the *"glorious riches of our His glorious inheritance"* (Ephesians 1:18 NIV). YHVH has a treasure chamber in his mountain administered by Melchizedek. Get your brain out of the poverty mindset. The real problem is the way we think.

YHVH Requires Faithfulness

"Moreover it is required in stewards, that a man be found faithful." (1 Corinthians 4:2 KJV)

The word *faithful* means to protect and maintain what you have in an excellent way, or to invest and become productive.

Do not take what YHVH has made you a steward of, and needlessly spend it on yourself. The Jewish culture encouraged investing a percentage of the parent's earnings as an inheritance for their children's children. They became productive with what they had. Be productive. Look at what you can do to reproduce what you receive and multiply it to make it better, not to desire more for the sake of more, but to make more to serve more.

You have got to understand these things that operate in the natural environment through the seven or eight families who control the finances of the earth. All their wealth will eventually be given to us if we can steward properly what He has given us. The Word says, *"The wealth of the Gentiles shall come to you... That men may bring to you the wealth of the Gentiles, And their kings in procession"* (Isaiah 60:5,11 NKJV). All the Lord is looking for are wise stewards who have become kings through stewardship and honour, and have learned to rule as sons. Then He can say to the foolish man over there, "You, all your money goes to him today! If you do not comply, you die and he gets it anyway. You choose!"

YHVH Rewards Good Stewards

"Well done.... I will make you ruler over many things..." (Matthew 25:21 KJV2000)

I do not think there has been anything more joyful for me than to hear the Father say, "Well done, son. Because you have ruled on this mountain, I have got other mountains that belong to you that are connected to your mountain, and now you can learn how to rule those as well."

The Lord delights in the prosperity of His sons and those who steward righteously. Look at David. It is estimated David gave about six billion dollars in today's money into the Temple. This is what David gave from his own personal wealth – not the kingly money, not the kingdom money, but his own personal money – for the building of the Temple.

David's mighty men are estimated to have given about a million dollars each. These were men who had nothing at their beginning with David. These men who were outcasts, became prosperous because of their union and connection to David. Now consider: where did that wealth come from? It came from them serving a king who served the Lord. Because he served the Lord, the glory came over him and became part of their blessing. They were able to sit in the shade of the tree that David had become.

As an owner of a business, if you do not steward your financial team and do not serve YHVH in all your financial arena, and if you have not walked out your life issues regarding stewardship, all those connected to you cannot be blessed. You will become the bottleneck for the blessing of the Father in your business and to all those around you. One of the key ingredients is to show yourself to be generous. Not to please the eyes of others but to please YHVH. The best practice is to do it "for the audience of one," in hiddenness and out of sight of everyone, so only YHVH sees. This blessing can then be filtered down into the arena of everything you touch. If you do not do this and steward rightly, if you serve yourself as an owner instead of serving YHVH as a steward, you will become the bottleneck stopping the overflow moving out to others.

Go: Ask Prudence

The Lord looks for opportunities to give increase to you and me out of stewardship. A functional part of that increase is to distribute witty inventions to us. Prudence is the being that dwells with the Spirit of Wisdom. By building a relationship with the spirit of Wisdom, we get access to engage with this being. The key is to ask out of relationship for witty inventions in everything you do to build increase. Prudence is found in Proverbs 8. *"I, wisdom, dwell with prudence..."* (Proverbs 8:12 NKJV). Prudence is a being, not simply the attribute of being prudent. Prudent describes someone's nature, but Prudence here in scripture is a sentient being who makes decisions on the distribution of witty inventions.

The point is, you have to say, "Prudence, thank you for witty inventions. Thank you for knowledge that gives me understanding about witty inventions, their application and how to build them. Even before this world was formed, you knew all about those inventions."

Keys to Stewardship

Poor stewards lose what they have, and the value of what is entrusted to them decreases. Stewards know what YHVH has entrusted to them, and they value it. They look all the time for opportunities to increase so that YHVH can benefit from them. They look at their possessions, their giftings, the truth, their callings, their relationships, and the words that have been spoken. Stewardship is a whole lifestyle that is not solely based on the structure of finances. Being a steward is all about serving the interests of another.

So how do I go from being a rich man to being a wise steward? Here are some keys that will be helpful in this issue.

- You must transition out of the negative environment you are used to, by changing your mindset, your thought processes and the desires of your heart.
- You need to clearly identify and acknowledge your weaknesses (particularly about the self, and the need for money) to be able to repent of them.
- If you think you are not well-off, find somebody who is less well-off than you. Live with them for a week and you will appreciate what you have.
- Realign your thinking to the Lord's way of thinking. Reset your desires to bring about new ones.
- Crucify the devourer of your emotions in the area of finances.
- Set your goals and live within a budget.
- Pray, pray, pray, pray, pray!

The key principle is to deal with the stronghold that identified you by what you have and do, instead of by who you are and will be.

Pressed Down, Shaken Together, Running Over

Much of the problem we have with the issue of money is our identification with the idea that "If I have money, I am going to look better, move faster, have better clothes, and a bigger car." That kind of thinking is all about self-identity. The Lord wants us to understand that it is not about us—it is about Him. He wants you to get to grips with the fact that He wants you to be free so that He can open up the windows of heaven to pour His blessing over your life, *"...pressed down, shaken together, and running over..."* (Luke 6:38 NKJV). My wife and I have covenanted not to have an open show or display of financial wealth. Having it is not the issue, it is what your heart does when you have it. Someone once said to me, "If you really want to know what is in a person give them power and money, then the truth will come out."

The Father wants to release to us and give us large portions like the cluster of enormous grapes, as the ones mentioned in Numbers 13:23. Have you ever wondered what those grapes were like for the children of Israel, when it took two men to carry one cluster of grapes? Let's say I can pick up about one hundred pounds. That means one cluster of grapes could have weighed two hundred pounds. That is colossal! Have you ever imagined biting into one of those grapes, and what it must have been like? For me, this is what the Father has in store for us.

I am telling you all this because YHVH is doing things we do not hear about. We do not hear about them because we are absorbed in the normal humdrum of life, instead of beginning to believe the Lord. I often find myself saying, "YHVH, You are doing something new in creation and I want part of it. Show me. Lord, let me wait in You. When I am waiting in You, I will be found in Your presence and You will show me the secret things, things locked up. Show me."

Deal with the motives of your heart. The Lord is more interested in the motives of your heart than in supplying you with billions and billions of dollars. If you can get the motives of your heart right, He will bless you in any way that is possible, any way He can. The Lord will do it. It is about adjusting the motives of your heart and adjusting the way that you think.

From Tens to Billions Via Purified Stewards

When I first got around some of these wealthy guys, I used to wrestle with tens of thousands of dollars. A hundred thousand dollars to me was a lot of money. It is a lot of money to someone who has nothing. A friend of mine who is in the top half-percent of earners in the United States would sit me down and talk money to me. He talked to me about hundreds of thousands of millions of dollars until I got used to talking about it.

When you are around the average person and you start talking about a million dollars, their eyes glaze over. Their heart and head have not expanded to the potential of what can be. When I spend time with those who talk billions and trillions of dollars, my brain stretches! YHVH wants to stretch our brain. A billion dollars is not a lot of money compared to the universe and all the solar systems that are in our awareness, including what is outside of the known universe. We have got to get our thinking right. Do not daydream about having millions of dollars. First, get your heart and the issue of stewardship right. Then allow the dreams to begin to grow, and get around people who say things that will stretch you.

YHVH is doing things with those who are becoming stewards. All He is looking for is where He can rest His head and who He can make a steward of the headship of the glory, because where the glory is, the gold will be found. The Father wants to get the vessel of silver made right, conformed right. He wants fire around the vessel of silver to purify it, to get all the dross out and make it float on the surface, just like oil does on water. The Father wants the vessel to be purified and sanctified. When it is, you can be set apart.

Your availability depends on the desires of your heart and the way you think. Of course, YHSVH is the true door into the

Father's house and Kingdom, and He will be the door that makes you available.

When the ancient ones came out of YHVH's realm, they did not just come out with a sword. They came out with a scale and they came out with gold. The scale is to balance and to see who is worthy of the gold that they brought out. The way you think and the issues in your heart will qualify you or disqualify you. YHVH wants to give back the treasures, treasures that flow out of the mountains of the dominion of YHVH Himself.

ACTIVATION

Father, today we lift our hands in surrender. YHVH, where I have been an owner and not a steward, today by faith I stand in the mobile court of Heaven and I repent. I agree with my adversary quickly. Father, I ask You to forgive me for having hidden desires in my heart that have not enabled You to bring blessing over my life. Today YHVH, in the scrolls of the courtroom of Heaven, let it be recorded that I repent. Father, there are records in my DNA that have made me think this way. I repent of them today. Father, I turn from money as my supply and the need for that supply. I turn to You as my supply. YHSVH, I turn to You as my head. Father, I allow You to come and rest Your head upon me. I set my thinking and my desires to be anchored on You as the owner and me as the steward. Father, I ask that Your fire would burn in my heart, to make me a wise steward of the things that You own. Train me and raise me as a wise son to be able to steward what You have delivered to me. I pray this in YHSVH's name. Amen.

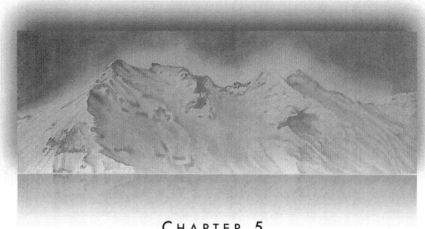

CHAPTER 5

POSITIONED

I want to talk about ascending because it is important we understand that spiritual engagement in our business life is not just about making ourselves feel good. It is not about stopping work for ten years to engage the Kingdom realms to try to become super spiritual.

Your engagement with your Kingdom life is experienced, not just done by separating yourself away from everything. What I have learned to do is to be able to go higher than the things that will keep me lower. When those things sit in front of us and engage us, I have learned to go higher. If it comes up then I go higher.

> *"But those who wait on the Lord Shall renew their strength; They shall mount up with wings like eagles, They shall run and not be weary, They shall walk and not faint."* (Isaiah 40:31 NKJV)

You will find that your stuff will only be able to go up to a certain height. Once it has reached its pinnacle you rise far above it.

The Word is very clear that we are to "...*Sit together in the heavenly places in Christ... far above all principality and power*" (Ephesians 2:6, Ephesians 1:21 NKJV). A heavenly place is a realm of rulership from where government is exercised. It is a realm where you and I have a position in Christ, because we are in Christ in heavenly places. Our big problem is that we have never been told we can go there. Nor have we been shown how to go there. So we will stay here, earthbound, while trying to bring resolution to the chaos that is here. When we do this from this position, we end up only supplying what is needed to maintain the chaos around us. The best way to deal with this kind of circumstance is to go higher above it, to purposely engage, being seated in Christ in that place high above it.

Going higher does not necessarily mean that I am going to be ascending up to the edge of the universe. It is a purposeful positioning into that heavenly place in Christ, a place where I observe the circumstance and the environment of its influence where chaos has been created. It is easy to have something that is a small thing shrouding your life and bringing its influence to bear by creating chaos, sitting over you like a blanket. If I were to move away from the shroud that is like a blanket and go above it, I would have a completely different perspective that is very helpful in solving chaotic issues. Often I would see it from this perspective as the small problem that it really is, because I have come above its influence. What I have learned to do is to remove myself from the vicinity of its influence and get away from what it is doing around my life, by going higher (Isaiah 40:31).

We are often taught in church to wait in this physical realm and become nice and still to try to hear the voice of YHVH instead of repositioning ourselves to see from His perspective.

Often familiar spirits have been in touch with our brokenness, and are directly involved in chaotic circumstances. They have the express purpose of keeping you under their control. When we are in that chaotic environment and try to bring resolution for it here without going into our heavenly seat, our familiar spirits can position themselves as an idol to speak to us in the same voice that YHVH does.[8] So you may think that it is YHVH. That is why verbal communication is not the highest form of communication. We have been told to "Hear the voice of YHVH" because He comes as "...*a still, small voice*" (1 Kings 19:12 NKJV). What I was not told is that we need to be up the mountain where the still small voice operates from first, to even be able to connect properly. YHSVH did not say, "I only do what I hear my Father saying." He said, *"I only do the works that I see the Father doing"* (John 5:19 TPT).

I was never taught how to go up the mountain to be an observer and to hear the *"still, small voice"* of the Lord. I was taught to stay here on the earth, at the bottom of the mountain, in this realm in the hope that I would hear something while trying to engage with the voice at the top. The key is that I was not interacting with Him on a personal level, positioned where He is. Did YHSVH say, "I only do what I hear my Father say?" No. Yet it has been taught like that as a doctrine in church and laid down as a foundation for us. YHSVH said He does only *"what He sees the Father do..."* (John 5:19 NKJV). The reason He could see what the Father was doing was because He was up the mountain. It is only when we are in the place of encounter that YHVH can come along beside us and speak to us. If you are in the right position, all He needs to do is talk to you in person, which is all about intimacy and relationship.

---

[8] See Chapter 3 on familiar spirits in *Realms of the Kingdom, Volume 2*. Available on sonofthunder.org.

His Fire and His Glory

The Word refers to *"They that wait upon the Lord..."* (Isaiah 40:31 KJ2000). We have been taught to sit here passively waiting. But *waiting upon the Lord* means an interactive, passionate pursuit with intent to position yourself in His realm to interface with Him. This is not a passive thing. It is an interactive, conscious decision. When you do this, it opens the way for you to ascend above your environment as on the wings of an eagle: *"But those who wait on the Lord shall renew their strength; they shall mount up with wings like eagles, they shall run and not be weary, they shall walk and not faint"* (Isaiah 40:31 NKJV). This is a place where you will not grow weary. It is not about our efforts, but about what He has done to accomplish on the earth what is needful, to position us in that place where we are able to engage with His fire and His glory. I am trying to unlock your thinking, because we need to get away from the normal religious understanding about waiting upon the Lord.

We are to present our bodies as living sacrifices. The Bible says, *"...present your bodies a living sacrifice, holy, acceptable to God, which is your reasonable service"* (Romans 12:1 NKJV).

The height, depth and breadth of your intimacy will dictate the height, depth and breadth of the encounter you will have with the person of YHVH – not just a voice. What I have found is that the framework of who I am as a being must be upon something other than myself.

The Bible talks about YHSVH being the Rock. Have you ever thought about what that rock would potentially look like? I like to consider the rock that followed the children of Israel in the wilderness, how it moved and what it looked like when it moved. Perhaps it moved like a caterpillar crawling along the ground. Maybe it wobbled when it moved. Maybe it floated! It is one of those things that has never been talked about, and the Word specifically says that it was Christ. *"For they drank of that spiritual Rock that followed them, and that Rock was Christ"* (1 Corinthians 10:4 NKJV).

Do you see how our brains work? There was a rock that followed them (the Israelites) in the wilderness. So YHSVH must be "a rock". Perhaps He is a lump of stone out there? Has anyone ever seen a lump of stone crawl around in the desert? No? That is because it was not a stone. The function of a rock is to provide a foundation of a history. The earth declares the glory of the Lord. The function of a rock is to show the history of the provision of YHVH to the earth. The provision of YHVH was seen in Israel when Moses smote the rock. The provision of YHVH was also revealed when Christ was crucified and walked through death to resurrection, to reveal the full provision of a new life. These two are linked.

The Bedouin tribes know how to find water in a rock. There is a special kind of rock which allows water to seep into the surface of the rock when it rains, and because of the mineral structure inside, the rock will form an outer layer under the surface. The water will not be released from the rock until you smash it. When you smash it the inside structure shatters and the water from the rock is released, but you will not normally get more than half a cup of water out of it.

The interesting thing was that this rock fed several million sheep, cattle and people. So the question to ask is, how big was that rock? We understand it as a supernatural supply – that was the miracle. You and I as living stones, given the example of YHSVH Himself, can also become a never ending supply of living water to the world that is around us.

> *"He who believes in Me, as the Scripture has said, out of his heart will flow rivers of living water."* (John 7:38 NKJV)

> *"He only is my rock and my salvation;*
> *He is my defense;*
> *I shall not be moved."* (Psalm 62:6 NKJV)

We are to stand on that rock (Matthew 7:24), which is also a coal of burning fire (Isaiah 6:6). The coal of burning fire is

YHVH's framework for our ability to ascend into His life and to be engaged and connected to Him. The Word says, "...*Who makes His angels spirits And His ministers a flame of fire*" (Hebrews 1:7 NKJV). How can you become a flame of fire unless you are identified with fire? Whatever you stand on will become the groundwork and the foundation for you to be nurtured by. Whatever nurtures you becomes the source of all that you will become like.

It is very important for us to engage in the process. We need to realise that we are the sacrifice (Romans 12:1). Sometimes our struggles within our pursuit of YHVH get affected by our soul and any hindrances and brokenness which reside in us. Sometimes the swirl of the environment that has created the issues around us will cloak and sit over us. When this cloaks us, it is important that we walk into the fire, stand on the rock, and allow the burning in the rock to consume us as a place of sacrifice. It is important that we move into the fire. By standing in the fire, it releases the potential for the cloaking, hindrances and brokenness to be destroyed.

Many of us excessively dislike fire and what it does because of our physical experience with fire on the earth. The fire of YHVH does not create death as fire does on the earth. Fire is a very interesting force. It changes the molecular structure of everything it touches. We only see the end product that it produces, not what goes on to create it. When the fire of YHVH comes around us, the purpose of that fire is to molecularly change us to be melded into something different. This is why it is important. Many of us are hesitant to go into fire because it will disrupt our ease and change our life, but it is a process and a process we often fight against.

So often when we are facing trials, either we will go through the fire or our "stuff" will speak to us. These internal voices of our familiar spirits are intent on keeping us distracted from what we should be doing, which is walking through the fire. The internal voices will say things like, "You are useless! You are a failure! This is not going to work! You cannot possibly solve those problems." The key response to these persistent voices is to go deeper into the fire, until all that is left is the burning love of YHVH. Walking this out is a journey that will bring maturity until all that is left is the record of YHVH burning in you. This will help the process of maturing you. YHVH is a consuming fire and you bear His image.

The fire of YHVH is an important reality that aids the process, the necessity is to understand that we will have to walk through the fire whether we like it or not. I have people coming to me and saying, "Ian, that was dealt with at the cross!" Often many of us do not realise that these battles go on unconsciously within us. The reality is we are still wrestling with the internal responses to those voices but do not recognise it. Sometimes I would just go and stand in the fire, just because I could and because I wanted to. Doing this will often provoke the reality of what is going on around me to be brought into the foreground, enabling me to see what I am really wrestling with.

In the Word there are two very succinct and important encounters regarding the fire, one with a furnace with Shadrach, Meshach and Abednego (Daniel 3:8–30 NKJV), and the other with some seraphim (Isaiah 6:1–6 NKJV). These two processes are important aspects for our lives, our willingness to go into the fire and to be purged in Heaven. They are directly related to us with regard to our functionality in the world around us.

We must be willing to run into the fire, instead of running away from it. Run through the fire with your troubles and allow the fire to trouble your troubles! Your troubles are actually not your own. You have made them but they are not yours. YHSVH is your burden bearer. YHSVH said, *"For My yoke is easy and My burden is light"* (Matthew 11:30 NKJV). You need to go into the fire.

> *"Therefore because the king's commandment was urgent, and the furnace exceedingly hot, the flame of the fire slew those men that took up Shadrach, Meshach and Abednego. And these three*

men, Shadrach, Meshach and Abednego, fell down bound into the midst of the burning fiery furnace." (Daniel 3:22-23 KJ2000)

Meshach, Shadrach and Abednego were bound and taken to the fiery furnace. The doors were opened and it says that the flames slew the soldiers that took them to the furnace. Therefore, there was no one to throw them into the fire. Yet the next verse says they were cast into the fire. This is evidence of people who were willing to cast themselves into the fire because they had already walked through it in their responses to Nebuchadnezzar. We need to be willing to throw ourselves into the fire of YHVH, as it may bring us the same results as these three men. The Word says their bindings were broken, they were walking freely and their clothes were not burned. Neither was there a smell of fire upon their heads (Daniel 3:27).

The question is, who cast them into the fire? Perhaps YHVH did? Fire is very important. When you go into it and engage with YHVH, the only things that will burn are the things that bind your life and stop you functioning. Everything that lives in you or that you have the capacity to live out but is not a binding, does not get touched. The Bible says not even a hair on their head was burned nor was there the smell of smoke on them. The only things that were burned were their bindings.

What is interesting is that it was the King who was accusing Meshach, Shadrach and Abednego, who went to the fiery mouth and said, *"...I see four men loose, walking in the midst of the fire; and they are not hurt and the form of the fourth is like the Son of God"* (Daniel 3:25 NKJV). The question is how did the King know what the Son of God would look like unless he had previously seen Daniel glorified? The next question to ask is where was Daniel? Perhaps he was already in the fire?

It was the King who bent down, called them out, and said, *"...There is no other God who can deliver like this"* (Daniel 3:29 NKJV). I have found that the issues we struggle with before we walk into the fire will often try to call us back or become a hindrance to us moving forward into the fire of YHVH. But when we come out of the fire, we come out victorious – we will come out ruling over the top of them, and over the top of the issues that created the circumstances around us. The fire is so important in this realm that we walk in, we must go into it. The key is to stay in the fire. When the chaos rages around me I make a conscious decision to walk into the midst of the fire of YHVH. I go there because that is my place of refuge. This is one of the secret places of YHVH that He has set up to be a refuge for us. Many people view this as a great place of trial. One of the reasons we go through trials is because we do not stand in the fire and allow it to do its job. YHVH has made it so much easier for us if we participate with Him. As scripture says, it is better for us to fall upon the rock than for the rock to crush us (Matthew 21:44). It does not matter what else gets burned. If it gets burned then it needed to burn and I would rather have it burn voluntarily than have YHVH come seeking to burn it. My attitude has always been, if I die, then I praise Him because I am dying in the best place I can – in His presence. *"For if we would judge ourselves, we would not be judged"* (1 Corinthians 11:31 NKJV).

This process of us engaging with the fire is important. I have spent hours sitting beside bonfires and watching coals of fire burning, cultivating the potential pattern and imagery of the physical reality of what fire looks like. I would then take those images in my memory and use them as a connection point through faith as a spiritual reality, and walk into them identifying that this is not there to destroy me but to intrinsically change everything around my life. Remember this was a journey that I chose to go on over a number of years to pursue the fire of YHVH, so that He could make me a flame of fire. *"And of the angels He says: 'Who makes His angels spirits and His ministers a flame of fire'"* (Hebrews 1:7 NKJV).

There is a fire that burns in the Kingdom realm of the earth and there is a fire that burns in the realm of Heaven. The connection point in the realm of Heaven is about the seraphim that Isaiah had an encounter with. Isaiah finds himself standing before YHVH and says, "...*Woe is me! for I am undone; because I am a man of unclean lips, and I dwell in the midst of a people of unclean lips...*" (Isaiah 6:5 KJ2000). The Bible says, "...*The seraphim flew to me, having in his hand a live coal which he had taken with the tongs from the altar...Your iniquity is taken away, And your sin is purged*" (Isaiah 6:7 NKJV).

I find this really weird because how can iniquity and transgression be in Heaven? In scripture it is written that YHSVH took His blood and cleansed the heavenly temple. *"Neither by the blood of goats and calves, but by his own blood he entered in once into the holy place"* (Hebrews 9:12, KJV). This was done specifically to deal with the yoke of Lucifer's trading to allow us unlimited access with all our brokenness to come into His presence. When we come there, with our record of corruption that has not gone through the fire here willingly, our iniquity cannot have influence or remain in Heaven because its ability to do this has been removed by YHSVH making it possible for us to come, by His blood. It means you can still take records of corruption there. It will not affect Heaven but you can still have them around you so that they can affect you here on the earth. It is the Father's desire that we are free from them. So when these things sit around me when I am in the presence of YHVH and I recognise them, I purposely turn to engage with the coals of the Seraphim that deal with the records of iniquity in my life.[9] This process is not just for your personal life but I have purposed it in a very similar way in my business life when I have found that there has been no other visible solution to conflict and chaos that has developed. I have found it very functional. The more you practise the easier it gets. The more persistent you are, the faster the process, especially when you do not know any other solutions.

---

[9] I have covered this in a teaching on the Seraphim which is available on my website: www.sonofthunder.org.

Engaging with the Spirit of Wisdom

One of the key ingredients for the way we operate in business is the need for wisdom in every choice we make, to reveal the glory of YHVH. This is very hard to do. Our biggest problem is that we do not have the wisdom we need because we do not go to the source of where to find it. The only way to find wisdom is to go to the source. She is called the Spirit of Wisdom. The Bible tells us, *"I wisdom dwell with prudence, and find out knowledge of witty inventions"* (Proverbs: 8:12 KJV). It is important for us to engage with the Spirit of Wisdom. Her main job is to teach us how to be His daily delight as we were at the beginning where she was. The Spirit of Wisdom is the one who can train you in this process.

> *"Then I was beside Him as a master craftsman;*
> *And I was daily His delight,*
> *Rejoicing always before Him,*
> *Rejoicing in His inhabited world,*
> *And my delight was with the sons of men"* (Proverbs 8:30–31 NKJV)

She is one of the Seven Spirits of God.[10] The Bible directs us how to find her.

> *"On the top of the heights beside the way, Where the paths meet, wisdom takes her stand; Beside the gates, at the entrance to the city, At the entrance of the doors, she cries out."* (Proverbs 8:2–3 AMP)

> *"She has slaughtered her meat, She has mixed her wine, She has also furnished her table."* (Proverbs 9:2 NKJV)

It is important that we pursue relationship with the Spirit of Wisdom with regard to our business and business life, and to get to know who she is as a being. Scripture tells us how to find her and how to engage with her. You can go through processes, actively engaging her in your life. This is so she will train you

---

[10] See *Realms of the Kingdom, Volume 1*, chapter 12 on the Seven Spirits of God. Available on sonofthunder.org.

and mentor you into who you really were, and who she knew you were, before you were on the earth. When you engage with her, a number of issues will come around your life. You will find that YHVH begins to bring and release things and ideas to you that most people would not think about.

The next thing I have found important is the place you position yourself. (Ian Johnson, a prophet from New Zealand, does a really good teaching this.)

I find it fascinating that we have been taught about doubting Thomas. It is really interesting that Thomas was the only one who put his hand into the side of YHSVH. Our Greek mindsets would have us think that YHSVH's wound is nice and healed and is now a scar and Thomas touched it. This is not what YHSVH said. He said, "...*Reach your hand here, and put it into My side...*"(John 20:27 NKJV). *Into* does not just mean touch on the outside. The first question I would ask is, "How come there was no blood there?" My second question would be, "What exactly did he touch?" Something really changed in his life when he engaged with it. He put his hand into the side of YHSVH in His resurrected state and reached into another dimension of life within the body of Christ. Through touching this dimensional life, he became so affected by it that this led to the biggest revival in India.[11] This revival occurred after Thomas put his hand in YHSVH's side.

It is recorded that in India Thomas sat for some time watching some people performing a sacrifice, throwing their oblation of water to their gods. He then walked out to the lake and said, "I do not think your god likes you because he is not receiving your sacrifice. The water is falling down again. My God likes

---

[11] "Modern Syrian Christians of Kerala [India]... believe that the Apostle Thomas—the one who so famously questioned Yeshua—visited here in A.D. 52 and baptized their forefathers ...to preach the Gospel." Paul Zacharia,"The Surprisingly Early History of Christianity in India." smithsonian.com. Feb 19, 2016. https://www.smithsonianmag.com/travel/how-christianity-came-to-india-kerala-180958117/

me and is superior to your god. He will receive my sacrifice and the water will stay in the air." So he collected some water and threw it into the air, and it stayed there. [12]

Positioning yourself is very important (some theologians call it posturing). That is the kind of thing that helps create a way for connectivity to YHVH. This helps us engage at an entry point with the realm of Heaven. Positioning for me is a combining together of my thoughts, my desires, my intents and my hopes to turn and focus them towards YHVH coming through my entry point of YHSVH. This helps me to find an entry point into the realm of Heaven. This develops the knowledge of access points through your participation that will eventually form an open gate to Heaven for you as an individual. The more time you spend actively participating in this process with the Father it develops an awareness of what I call the ebb and flow of the emotions of Heaven. It increases your awareness of Heaven itself and your capacity to maintain your connectivity to it, increasing your ability to feel when you cross over, where the realm of the presence of Lord becomes real. You can feel or sense it around you and know that this is the crossover point. Once this crossover point has been identified, that becomes our identified place of beginning. The more I practise going in and out of this, positioning myself in and out of that gate, the faster my access becomes in and out until it becomes a subconscious lifestyle of pursuit.

One of the things that I have purposed to do in my business life, whether I am at work or not, is when I begin to get stressed, I walk into the fire by faith. I engage by using the crossover point to bring an awareness of the presence of YHVH into my environment, and shift my focus from what is happening onto Him. I go through those processes and then I sit in the gate. Instead of listening to the stressful raging of the voices

---

[12] See Matthew Bryan. "Exploits of the Apostle Thomas in India." Conciliar Post. April 4, 2017. https://conciliarpost.com/christian-traditions/exploits-apostle-thomas-india/.

that are around me, it refocuses and reconnects me into the source of supply that is found in YHVH. Through this I am now turning my heart towards the presence of YHVH. That is what repentance is. Repentance is not repeating, "I am sorry, I am sorry." That is our Greek mentality and what we have been taught in church. Repentance is an act of turning towards the wonderment of who YHVH is, turning back to the perfect state of awe in Him.

Our position therefore is very important. What I have learned to do is to purpose to stand in that gate, no matter what goes on around me, or what is happening in the atmosphere around my life. This is not a formula with consecutive steps one to ten where, if I follow the steps, then X will happen for me. It all comes down to relational union with YHVH. Out of that relationship, I position myself by doing these things because it helps to engage the intimacy that the relationship brings. Please do not try to follow a formula and avoid the relationship. Part of our biggest problem is that we want formulas but we do not want the relationship.

When the stress is around me in my businesses, workplace or at home, I make a choice to consciously and continually turn my heart to engage the presence of YHVH at the crossover point, where He meets me. I try and stay there through my day. I open the latticework of my heart, and I try to engage that process to stay in connection with the presence of YHVH (Song of Solomon 2:9). He is interested in what I am doing as I walk with Him in my realm through my day.

There are two places you can walk with the Father. One is in His realm with Him doing His stuff and the other is with Him in your realm while you do your stuff. Both are important. YHVH wants to share life with you here (on earth) as much as He wants you to share His life with Him there (in Heaven). I have found that going and being an observer and learning how to participate, becoming a functional part of what goes on in Heaven helps me to engage with the protocol of His life in His

Kingdom. This helps to teach us to become a participant in the many functional ways that Heaven operates in, that are derived through relationship with YHVH.

I have found that positioning has been very important with regard to relationship; opening my heart, entering those arenas and keeping the relationship alive. When I do that, I have found that it aids me to begin to receive inside knowledge about what is going on within my businesses or the areas I am focused on. Remember this practise regarding business is only one part of the whole. I do this with my family, with finances, with friends, with relationships , etc. I first learned to do this with my family. I would go away for so much of the year I had to hold them in my heart, overshadow them and pray over them. Not to demand what I thought they needed to be doing, but to allow my heart, through connection with YHVH, to love them, yearn over them and desire the best for them. I would watch over them and try to get a feeling for where they were at. I was not even consciously trying to figure out how to be there from where I was, overseas, actively engaging with them. It is interesting to note that even YHSVH said, *"Where I am you may be also"* (John 14:3). This helped me to position myself where they are also. This is not using astral projection to try and make another person do what I want them to do. This is being hidden in YHVH to the point where you get lost in what He wants for their life. So that through that, your longing and your desires for them, for what YHVH has wanted, develops. It is interesting that wherever YHSVH is, I am there in Him. If I am in Him and He is omnipresent, then wherever He is, I can be there also."*...I am in My Father, and you in Me, and I in you"* (John 14:20 NKJV).

I found that by engaging like that within my business, made my business a part of my life. My business was not something I did. Engagement with YHVH in my business is who I am. It became a place of consecration and a place of encounter with the presence of the Lord. Therefore I could rejoice in my office.

I could rejoice in my car, my garden, at home, travelling around with my family, sleeping in bed or in a plane travelling to and from nations. It was all in my heart. By overshadowing and engaging my business, I found that I could look into my businesses and begin to see what was physically going on with staff, circumstances and within the environment of the business. YHVH would download and give me inside information on how to bring resolution to situations without being there. It was so much easier doing it this way and getting inside information, than spending all hours trying to figure out solutions.

It is being spiritual in every environment in my life, not just in my free time with YHSVH at home in the middle of the day. Standing in some of those positions has been very important for me, particularly in regard to maintaining a flow of relationship with the Lord in my business, in my family home, in my preaching life, in my spirit life and in relationships in life with other people.

The Heavenly Ecclesia

Your ecclesia or your senior leader does not rule over you or control you or your business life. When you are in a body of people in which you have chosen to base yourself, you are there to serve that body of people with what YHVH has given to your life. When you are actively participating in meetings in that body or environment itself, you serve that body of people with all that YHVH has given you, engaging with their authority and government to increase the corporate union. When you are not in meetings within that platform or body life, it has no influence or authority over your life in any form whatsoever. Remember, it is a choice to serve and you are there in a voluntary capacity. Oftentimes this is completely forgotten by many in leadership. Outside of that ecclesia or body of people, that government is not your covering, YHSVH is. Relational connection and union with one another on the earth is the primary place of correction, where iron sharpens iron and is one of the most vital ingredients to maturity. *"As iron sharpens iron, so a man sharpens the countenance of his friend"* (Proverbs 27:17 NKJV). This is the place within relationships – I am not talking about task orientated relationships, but personal relationships – where the deeper stuff of life can begin to get exposed. Basically, this is where your stuff gets exposed in a loving way, so it can be dealt with properly. I do not believe in "lone rangers," that is someone who is an island and completely isolated.

Accountability in every aspect and area of life is important for us as human beings. Oftentimes I find the system has taken that place, enforcing accountability through task orientation instead of relationship. This is why our relationship with YHVH is as important as relationships within humanity. You cannot say you love YHVH when you do not love others (1 John 4:20). I have found that when people are broken they will isolate themselves to control their environment and others around them, so that their own life does not have to be looked at. It is amazing how even in business life you find this amongst staff. This is all part of humanity that we need to be dealing with. This dealing does not only take place in an ecclesiastical environment but also in business life. I personally set about training my staff how to relate and communicate in a viable, relational, honest way with integrity and honour, both with one another and with me as their boss.

People say to me if you do not go to church you are not really a believer. It all depends on what church you are looking at. Do you mean that body of people that gather on the face of the earth on a Sunday, or those that gather together in Heaven every day, or those that are in relational connection with one another on a regular basis? There is a wider body that also includes the Men in White Linen, the Spirits of Just Men Made Righteous, the Ever Living Ones, the Men of Old, the Desert Fathers etc. that are also part of an ecclesia that we have the capacity to gather with. These are all part of the Greater Cloud of Witnesses. We are the ones that have put the delineation mark between what is spiritual and what is earthly. We have called one material (the earthly – the church) and the other immaterial, (heavenly – the Greater Cloud of Witnesses) when really one (heavenly) is more important than the other (the earthly). My relationship with the Men in White Linen is as important as my relationship with people here on the earth. Those of the Greater Cloud of Witness have a bit more life experience than most people down here, considering that some of them have been alive for two thousand years!

Stewarding Finances

The Old Testament perspective of finances was that you own everything you have. Out of your love for YHVH you give Him ten percent of everything, including ten percent of the spoils and everything you earn. This is called a tithe, which is ten percent. The Old Testament view is to tithe your way to the good kind of life. Receiving the tithe or that ten percent is commonly done in churches every week as an offering in the church system. This is really a good way for the church to budget. I was part of a church board for twenty years and became very familiar with the mathematics of how to work out your budget based on the number of people you have in your church. You know that when you have five hundred people in your church and the average family in the demographic you are in earns forty-five thousand dollars per annum, ten percent of forty-five thousand dollars multiplied by five hundred is approximately two hundred and twenty-five thousand dollars per annum. You can work your budget out by binding people to ten percent of their earnings. This is Old Testament thinking, tithes and offerings that completely lacks the connection to responding to YHVH's heart. This is a slave mentality where there is no need to have relational connection with YHVH because you are living by a law. Churches will very often have special offerings to meet other needs as required.

The New Testament perspective is gifts and giving. YHVH owns it all and you ask Him how much you give. He has given it to me and I am to be a good servant. Is being a good servant giving just ten percent? Perhaps what YHVH is asking you to do is to go beyond the comfort bounds of the religious system that we have been tied into. *"But others fell on good ground and yielded a crop: some a hundredfold, some sixty, some thirty"* (Matthew 13:8 NKJV). The New Testament, through gifts and giving, teaches you how to live the acceptable kind of life. This contrasts with the Old Testament which teaches you to live the good kind of life.

The most amazing thing I have found is that it can sometimes take thirty-five years to begin to reap from tithing. This changes as we develop into gifts and giving, through being a servant of YHVH to complete stewardship as a son. Stewardship as a son is aligned to living the perfect kind of life. It is an empowered life that is governed by relationship. Our connection with what we have is based around stewardship, where YHVH owns it, you are responsible to Him for all of it; to keep it, to multiply it and be completely responsive to what He wants. Here is where we ask Him how much we keep, not how much we give. This goes way beyond the ten percent as a slave. I have found personally that YHVH has always challenged me to err on the side of abundance in giving and complete generosity.

Financial integrity is definitely important to Holy Spirit. Even if we have financial difficulties through making some mistakes or things mess up around you that are out of your control, hold on to your integrity the best way you can. Dealing with everything with integrity is important. You will find that YHVH will engage with you and will bring you to a point where you can begin to see your way out of these difficulties. There have been times in my own personal life where things have been messed up badly. It is important to maintain integrity, engage with people, talk with them and communicate with them. Do not withdraw from them, keep it open. Integrity is important in all your business dealings.

As a businessperson I find it very hard to employ Christians. This is mostly because my experience has been that many of them seem to lack integrity in work ethics. Oftentimes I have also found them to be lazy. Somehow they seem to think that as a fellow believer, you will tolerate more than is acceptable. It is almost like they think that we owe them something. Another aspect I have found with believers, especially in business to business with other believers, is that sometimes Christians do not like paying their bills – especially if you are a believer and they owe you money. This is absolutely weird to me, how this goes on within the body life. I know that if I hate it, YHVH hates it as well. This seems to come out of the thinking to forgive your brother his debts instead of the thinking that a labourer is worthy of his hire. This is where the mentality of everything should be free comes from, when it is based around anything to do with YHVH. This is directly connected to a slave mentality and generally based around irresponsibility.

One thing I have had to learn in dealing with Christians is what I call "a big stick theology" – you get your big stick out, you beat them, and you hold them to account the same way YHVH holds us to account for being a good steward of all that He owns. I have found it helpful at times to be confrontational about bad debts. To be able to deal with this properly, we must set an example in our life of someone who always pays their debts on time and when needed. It has often been useful to get on the phone and be a tough love Christian. It is important that believers are held to account for their bad debts. Even Christ made references in some of His parables to the way the Father responds to people who are not good stewards. YHVH uses tough love as well when He has to.

My awareness of YHVH and my love for Him over-rides everything that I do, and must overshadow everything that I touch. The preparation of maintaining the state of overshadowing without having business pressure helps me to be fore-armed, so that when pressure comes on me, it is much easier to handle in the business environment. When the pressure comes on, I begin to purposefully engage into that realm as I have already learned the pattern through practise when there was no pressure, training my responses to build neural pathways and records into my mind and my DNA.

Practicing these things is important. It is not something that comes just because you come to a business meeting with Ian Clayton or read a book. You cannot suddenly think it is all going to be great without practise. I have never found that this process has come by impartation. The information has come through listening or reading, but practise formulates the process. I have never found in the Bible that YHVH said that it would be easy. I find that what He does say is that we will overcome. *"He who overcomes shall inherit all things, and I will be his God and he shall be My son"* (Revelation 21:7 NKJV).

It is also important for us to realise that as believers in business we are viewed as weird by the world. One of the traditional belief systems regarding abundance or having an overflow of abundance is that we are supposed to live our life through a lifestyle of poverty, as if it is morally good to live in poverty. This implication is such wrong thinking as far as I am concerned in business life. As a steward I want to increase that which I am accountable for. I really believe peoples' mentality about this issue of poverty is changing the way that business functions on the face of the earth today. I believe that there is a kingly realm that YHVH wants to instigate for Kingdom people. The reality is that there could be such an overflow that there is more than sufficient for everything as YHVH has need. If YHVH has called you into this arena as an act of sacrifice rather than a place of slavery and bondage to poverty, that can be a beautiful thing.

I believe that our mentality about what YHVH has given us has got to change. Our thinking has to change from slavery, into stewardship, and then sonship as an co-owner. Being a steward of what YHVH has given us is vital for increasing our level of responsibility, which increases our level of abundance. Your internal reactions will show you where your maturity is regarding this issue of poverty. The first time someone asks you how come you are living in abundance, it will challenge and reveal exactly where you are at regarding your belief systems and how you feel about abundance. However, I do not believe personally in the opulent display of wealth in normal circumstances.

I play golf with a specific friend of mine. It is one of the easiest places to lose your cool, especially when someone is watching! Sometimes when you try to make a good shot, the ball does not do what it is supposed to do. One of the funniest things I have ever experienced has been on the golf course, in front of the clubhouse. I was going to drive off the first tee, I hit the ball which hit a woman's tee. That caused the ball to fly back into the veranda of the clubhouse, bounce up and down in front of the clubhouse and finally bounce back down to the tee from where I had hit it. A man spoke over the loud speaker saying, "I think the fairway is the other side!" It is amazing to watch your responses and your emotions during this type of circumstance in life, when you think you have it right and it does not quite go the way you want it to go.

Maturity in Integrity

When you go through life, enjoy the journey. Do not try to find short cuts or hurry it. The things I practice within my businesses have laid a foundation so that I can engage new and greater things. Maintaining your integrity in your decisions and responses is vital. This is both in your thought life and in your actions. I can remember going through circumstances in my life where things were not very nice. I can remember shaking the hand of someone, saying, "Nice to see you" and praying in tongues, fighting with myself on the inside. I found that the internal triggers of my own personal life show me the level of maturity that I have maintained in my connection with the Kingdom world. When I find these things and respond in the right way, then I know that I am ready to go higher. Until these circumstances generate the right responses inside us, we cannot try to go to the next level. It is best to work through how you have responded and learn new ways of responding. If you are working through something in your life, enjoy where you are because when it passes, there will be greater responsibility. It is the same in your business. When you are going through stages in your business, try to work through the struggle, the heartache and the pain to get there. *"We know that all things work together for good to those who love God, to those who are the called according to His purpose"* (Romans 8:28 NKJV). None of it will be wasted. YHVH will always use adverse circumstances to help us along the journey, especially when we think we have nothing wrong. You cannot suddenly arrive at maturity. You need to be matured, particularly in business.

The reason I teach so much about money is because it is very important. I really do believe that YHVH is going to unlock the realm of overflowing abundance. I believe there will be a time when there is a never-ending bowl of supply that YHVH is going to release to His sons. He is looking for people who have gone through the hard knocks of life. People who have walked some of this out, who are not afraid to get into the face of some of it and just stand in the strength that YHVH has given them. The Word says, *"You therefore must endure hardship as a good soldier of Jesus Christ"* (2 Timothy 2:3 NKJV) It is this process of learning how to walk through, never losing your union with YHVH and overcoming, that qualifies us for this never ending supply. Everything was only ever promised to them that overcome. This is important for what we will be doing in the future. That way, when the over abundant supply is released, it has a sure foundation to rest on and will not destroy your life. One of the key components to qualifying in anything with YHVH is overcoming. Learning how to stand in adversity and never wavering, builds iron in our constitution that becomes foundational. I have found there are many people who have never learned how to have a disciplined enduring lifestyle, who want the overflow. Many have been talking about it but will not necessarily see it.

Character Versus Nature

Many of us have heard that when it gets tough, the tough get going. That is true but it is not all the truth. Your character is not revealed when it gets really tough, your nature is revealed. Your character gets revealed by your response when you are given too much. It is our character that YHVH wants to develop in us, and it is our nature He wants to mature. Your nature is connected to your thoughts and your character is connected to your intentions. The Bible says His word is *"...Sharper than any two-edged sword, piercing even to the division of soul and spirit, and of joints and marrow, and is a discerner of the thoughts and intents of the heart"* (Hebrews 4:12 NKJV). Look at what is in your life, as this will be helpful to you in your walk with YHVH.

These things are not easy, and they have not been easy for me. I have found that the more I persistently engage this area and get into the realm where the glory of God is found inside Christ, the easier it gets. *"Therefore, if anyone is in Christ, he is a new creation; old things have passed away; behold, all things have become new"* (2 Corinthians 5:17 NKJV). Grace is not a theology for the tolerance of sin. Grace is the empowerment of YHVH for us to walk according to His power and His will. This means that we need to establish our land and boundaries. When YHVH presented the promised land to the children of Israel He said to them, *"I will not drive them out from before you in one year; lest the land become desolate, and the beasts of the field multiply against you"* (Exodus 23:29

KJ2000). YHVH said, *"Little by little I will drive them out from before you..."* (Exodus 23:30 KJ2000) I have found that to be the same in the things we have been talking about. All of these are little by little, increments that actually open up the door for us to experience something that is far bigger and will have a far greater effect than the reality of what we currently walk in.

I am aware that some of us are in the middle of really tough trials. Maybe you are looking for breakthrough or even enjoying the journey you are on. Incrementally changing as you move forward is important in learning how to overcome. I really love the statement, "You can eat an elephant, one bite at a time!" Some of us just have to start eating. I never try to find a way out, I just try to find a way through.

When YHVH tries your character, do not hide. When the hand of YHVH comes upon your life and you want to run, go deeper. When you find He has got His sword out and He is circumcising your heart, allow Him to do it. Do not hide behind the protective mechanisms of race, creed, colour or your position in society. You have to allow YHSVH to do what He needs to do in you because it is maturity that He wants. When He matures you on the inside, He will show you on the outside as a mature being, who can handle the responsibility of what is coming to mankind/humankind.

What would you do if YHVH gave you one hundred thousand dollars? Pay off debt? Buy a car? What would you do if YHVH gave you one hundred million dollars? Pay off debt? Buy a car? Buy a boat? Maybe give some away? What would you do if YHVH gave you ten billion dollars? Buy a bigger car? More cars? A bigger boat? A bigger house? A beach somewhere and give some away? What would you do if He gave you one hundred billion dollars? Buy a bigger house and land with a garage and fill it with cars, buy a golf course and play golf, maybe give some away? What would you do if He gave you one trillion dollars? Buy a really big house? Buy New Zealand? Feed some poor? Buy a bigger boat? And maybe buy half the coastline of England? The real question that YHVH is looking for is inside your heart. Does it own you or do you own it? If you own it then you will be a steward of it. If it owns you then it will control you and it will demand from you. It will eat you up and it will spit you out the other side.

Building Your Mountain

I have had people tell me that they are going to go into the financial mountain, one of the seven mountains that is being taught. I do not know about you, but I do not want a seeded mountain that has been built by men of renown. People say they are going to go into a mountain and are going to take over that mountain. They are going to become part of that mountain and are going to begin to engage that mountain. But that whole mountain has been built out of corruption. The foundation of it is corrupt. The mountain is corrupt, so if you go into corruption to deal with corruption by corruption, corruption is all you are going to get.

Instead of trying to go into a mountain, build a completely new one. Allow YHVH to build around you what He needs to, so that you can establish what He wants on the earth. Not by using what man has established by building a false tower into the realms of the spirit world, trying to fulfil his own needs by sitting on top of the mountain. I am not one that really likes all those teachings on the seven mountains. Our objective is to build our own mountains, not to occupy one that has already been built. Our focus is not on my career pathway to be able to enter a mountain that is already there. My object for my life is to engage with the blueprint of YHVH's mountain and facilitate its administration on the earth to build a copy of it here. One of the key components to developing what YHVH wants in creation is not to study what is in creation and try to bring YHVH into it. It is about observing what He is doing and how His world functions, and then learning how to facilitate and administrate that out here in creation. It is a shame that very little knowledge about YHVH's mountain has been taught. This knowledge of what His mountain is like will very slowly come to the fore. In the last eight years, for me personally, I have taught many pieces of revelation about YHVH's mountain. Your heart will be the first thing the Father will deal with. If the mountain of your heart is not sorted, you are not going to be able to facilitate the reality of what YHVH wants here in creation.

CHAPTER 6

GOVERNMENT OF THE SEAT OF REST

The Government of the Seat of Rest is the domain of the Kingdom that operates through our life from the place of rest. YHSVH said, *"Take My yoke upon you and learn from Me, for I am gentle and lowly in heart, and you will find rest for your souls. For My yoke is easy and My burden is light"* (Matthew 11:29-30 NKJV). Rest does not mean lying on our bed. Rest means being still in a place, in absolute peace, even when tumult is all around our life. A good scriptural example of this is when YHSVH and the disciples were in the boat on the Sea of Galilee during a storm.

> *"Now when He got into a boat, His disciples followed Him. And suddenly a great tempest arose on the sea, so that the boat was covered with the waves. But He was asleep. Then His disciples came to Him and awoke Him, saying, 'Lord, save us! We are perishing!' But He said to them, 'Why are you fearful, O you of*

little faith?' Then He arose and rebuked the winds and the sea, and there was a great calm. So the men marveled, saying, 'Who can this be, that even the winds and the sea obey Him?" (Matthew 8:23-27 NKJV)

There was thunder, lightning, and big waves all around them. His disciples were freaked out, yet YHSVH was sleeping. We read that they came and shook Him, asking if He cared about them. While they felt like they were dying, YHSVH stilled the storm.

The Government of the Seat of Rest produces the power that comes with rest and the authority to function out of that rest. Therefore, it is important for us to understand how to find rest. The Seat of Rest is not in the Heavens; that is where we find peace. The Seat of Rest is within our temple. YHSVH said, *"For indeed, the Kingdom of God is within you"* (Luke 17:21 NKJV). The Kingdom of God is a manifestation of the fullness of the Government of YHVH within us. It brings revelation of that Kingdom, administrating it into the world around us, out of the place of the seat of rest. When I began to realise there was something the Father was trying to speak to me about, I would spend my mornings engaging the Seat of Rest. As I began to pray, the Lord would speak to me about sitting on the Seat of Rest, with me as a being, being empowered to express the Government of Rest from the Seat of Rest. The seat releases power when arcing with us, when we sit on it. We need the union between the seat and ourselves for our position to function in rest. We arc with our Seat of Rest as an expression of the Government of YHVH.

When I was in Jakarta, I was taken to the place where the king's seat was. It was a great big throne. I climbed up on the seat and sat there. As I did, I surveyed all around me. It was a wonderful experience that gave me an anchor for a testimony of reality. When I sat on the seat, I could survey, not just a part, but everything that was going on around it. I thought this would be an experience I could use when I got home. Once home, I got my chair and put it in my room. I prayed to Father, thanking Him that I could sit on the Seat of Rest. I was sitting on my chair, but in my hidden heart, I was climbing onto that big throne. "Father, I sit here on the Seat of Rest by faith in Christ. I sit on it, in the name of YHSVH." I then began to speak into my business, "Father, out of the Seat of Rest, I bring the Government of the Kingdom to bear over my work, into my work environment, and all the domain You have given me, over which I have authority. From the Seat of Rest, I look into my business and administrate this government into my work today from the Seat of Rest; and I command everything to be subject to this realm of the Kingdom." I went to work that day and accomplished in only two hours what would normally have taken eight hours to do. As an example of this, I had thirty-two staff, whose timesheets would normally have taken me eight hours to figure. I suddenly found I could do them in an hour and a half.

I started experimenting for a week. Suddenly, I had all this time on my hands. Forty hours' worth of work was done in eight hours. I decided I was going to push at this. For three or four weeks I engaged it seriously, sitting down and engaging this Kingdom realm. By the end of that four week period, I was doing in an hour what would have taken me eight hours. Suddenly, everything around me was working and readjusting itself, under this form of government that I had found a way to express and administrate into the world around me. When problems arose, I would sit on my Seat of Rest by faith, activating my memory of what I had been practising at home. (By now, I had been at this for six months. This does not just happen because we do it once or twice. We must practise it, over and over, to build retentive memory patterns; and practise this way of the Kingdom). I would embrace the problem, bring it into my heart, and sit over it, administrating rest into it and into the environment surrounding it from the Seat of Rest. I would bring my thoughts, engage the Scriptures, and bring them to bear over the top of it. The same way as you would put a rain coat on, from the Seat of Rest, I would cloak that environment. I found that it became an easy way to fix some of the things that were troublesome. I would often find answers by viewing the environment from the Seat. When I would see those answers, I would go and do what I saw. This was an unfolding of the environment, to give me wisdom on how to appropriate what I was observing through the process that I just mentioned above. I would go and do it. Just remember, everything administrated through you, out of this realm of the Kingdom, that comes into the earth, the earth is subject to it. This was the beginning of my journey into understanding and unlocking the provision of the Seat of Rest.

The Seat of Rest is inside of us. It is an expression of your government. As a king and a son, we are mandated to sit on the Seat and learn how to understand it and its function. The key is surrendering that Seat to another, which is Christ, to be trained in how to govern and administrate from it. For us to come into the revelation of the Kingdom, we must first learn how to surrender to the provision of salvation. We must bring Christ into the centre of our life and acknowledge what He did, to redeem us from the power of sin. The key here then is to abdicate the throne of your heart to Christ within your life. We cannot assume any form of Government until we have abdicated that throne to Him. In surrendering to Him, He can set Himself to train us how to express government through His life and what His expectations are. Again this is a process that takes time, it does not happen overnight.

It is by surrendering to lordship that we learn how to become a lord. Trained in what to do and not do, we learn how to function as a king. YHSVH then gets us ready to step up a level, so we can assume responsibility for our life. He steps up into Kingship, so that we become lords by being trained in how to become kings. The Seat of Rest is the beginning of the training that YHVH has in order for us to become kings. This realm of lordship is also the realm of functionality of the priesthood, where we learn what it is to be a priest of YHVH, administrating the priestly duties of the Kingdom on the face of the earth. It is not until we assume the seat, that we begin to rule properly over the domain of our body and the atmosphere that is immediately around us. Before we can rule in the area YHVH has given us, we have to submit to His rulership.

Let us go through a few more scriptures here.

"Now God has offered to us the same promise of entering into his realm of resting in confident faith. So we must be extremely careful to ensure that we all embrace the fullness of that promise and not fail to experience it." (Hebrews 4:1 TPT)

"For those of us who believe, faith activates the promise and we experience the realm of confident rest!" (Hebrews 4:3 TPT)

The whole of the Throne Room in Heaven shuts down every seven days. The Governmental realm of the Throne of YHVH shuts down. Everyone can go into the Kingdom realm and have fellowship together with one another in the houses of the Father while He is not sitting on His governmental seat. Remember, He walked in Eden to fellowship with Adam off His throne. You cannot have fellowship and build relationship while He is sitting on His throne administrating everything. We are all living stones, and in our relational connection with one another, we build a house. We come together to celebrate the realm of the Kingdom with us on that day of rest. We worship and celebrate YHVH while we are together in His presence. As He rested on the seventh day, we are in the seventh day now. This is the day of YHVH's rest when we should be coming into the place of Government to assume the role of responsibility.

"Those who first heard the good news of deliverance failed to enter into that realm of faith's-rest because of their unbelieving hearts. Yet the fact remains that we still have the opportunity to enter into the faith-rest life and experience the fulfillment of the promise!" (Hebrews 4:6 TPT)

"Now if this promise of "rest" was fulfilled when Joshua brought the people into the land, God wouldn't have spoken later of another "rest" yet to come. So we conclude that there is still a full and complete "rest" waiting for believers to experi-

ence. As we enter into God's faith-rest life we cease from our own works, just as God celebrates his finished works and rests in them. So then we must give our all and be eager to experience this faith-rest life, so that no one falls short by following the same pattern of doubt and unbelief." (Hebrews 4:8–11 TPT)

"For the word of God is living, and powerful, and sharper than any two-edged sword, piercing even to the dividing asunder of soul and spirit, and of the joints and marrow, and is a discerner of the thoughts and intents of the heart." (Hebrews 4:12 KJ2000)

The foundation of YHVH's rest is found in three things in this verse: the Word of YHVH, the piercing and dividing of the joints and the marrow, and discerning of the thoughts and intents of the heart. The Government of the Seat of Rest is the protocol by which those three things come to pass in our life. The joints and the marrow are very important because the joints give the body the ability to move; going in and out, to and fro, and up and down. The marrow speaks of the record. The word of YHVH comes in and pierces into the record of what we are doing and into our movements, so that record submits to something higher than itself. The next one is the discerner of the thoughts and intents of our heart. When the word of YHVH comes, Lordship comes and begins to sort out our heart, causing it to submit its thoughts and intents to YHVH's Government. When these three things are operational in our life, we will find rest.

YHSVH did not strive about anything. In fact, everything that YHSVH did, He did out of rest. As a thirteen year old boy sitting down in the temple, he expounded on the Kingdom with the doctors of the law. Everything came out of rest. What did YHSVH say when His mother and father came to Him? *"Did you not know that I must be about My Father's business?"* (Luke 2:49 NKJV). All of which came out of the Seat of Rest. When we are about the Father's business, we will find rest in everything we do. If we are about our own business, then we will find that we will strive for everything. And when we strive, we get half of the work done, and it takes us twice the amount of time to do it. YHVH wants us to enter into rest, so He can empower us to govern all that is around us that is out of rest.

It is about surrender. Everything comes back to relational surrender to the person called YHSVH, so He can become Lord, and then King, to train us to become lords and kings. He will train us to become a lord of lords and a king of kings, to take our position in the realm of Heaven. Everything is about maturity – going forward and expressing the Government of YHVH's Kingdom, moving up in responsibility, provision, authority and dominion. This is why YHSVH could say, *"All authority has been given to Me in heaven and on earth. Go therefore... I am with you always, even to the end of the age"* (Matthew 28:18-20 NKJV). No striving. Everything has already been done and completed. "You go... and I am with you." Rest does not mean not doing anything. Rest is when we are in the turmoil of life, in the middle of it, we can find this rest from that seat, so that the government will come to reign through peace.

The way Solomon reigned in peace was not through war, but in rest. Out of this rest, he established a whole nation that became the provision for all the kings of the earth who came to trade with him.

The key principle of understanding Rest is to understand the realm of the government of YHVH, whose authority and power function within that realm. The Kingdom has a ruler - a King who has absolute power and dominion over all the areas of responsibility given to Him.

> *"Now is the time for us to progress beyond the basic message of Christ and advance into perfection. The foundation has already been laid for us to build upon: turning away from our dead works to embrace faith in God"* (Hebrews 6:1 TPT)

When we try to rescue ourselves, or create self-efforts, we are creating a dead work. Dead works can be anything, even healing the sick, if that is not written in our scroll. It is awesome to heal the sick and raise the dead. It is a gift that is given to us for a specific purpose in the midst of a circumstance, in which the Father wants to meet another's need. The gifts that flow out of our life are not supposed to bring us affirmation. They come out of relationship with the presence of the Holy Spirit, where YHVH wants to meet another's need through our life. We just happen to be the right channel for it. We must not get our affirmation from the function, the operation, or the manifestation of the gifts of the Holy Spirit. Our affirmation must come out of our relationship with YHVH.

In a natural kingdom, a king has dominion and rulership over the extent of his government, which is called his kingdom. The Kingdom of Heaven, which is above, and the Kingdom of God, which is in us, create a platform for us to be ruling through maturity as Lords and Kings. We can rule over the domain and be the extension of YHVH's government into the realm of the earth. A kingdom requires that we have dominion within ourselves to rule over our life first. This is the key to literally coming to maturity: learning how to govern yourself, before you try to govern your environment or others. Remember, dealing with your stuff is the key to maturity. This enables us to be able to assume responsibility for our life, and bring direction to it, under the hand and shadow of YHVH.

Rulership is all about submission and the desire to serve the will of another. The way we learn about lordship is the same way YHSVH did. *"Father, if you are willing, take this cup of agony away from me. But no matter what, your will must be mine"* (Luke 22:42 TPT).

YHSVH could have walked away from the cross. He could have asked the Father for a legion of angels to deliver Him right then, and it would have been done. If He had walked away from His purpose on earth, there would have been no salvation for humanity. All of creation is groaning for our revealing as a son of God, and for our establishment of correct rulership, in a divine way, through maturity. Creation needs to be able to sit under our shadow in the same way we learn to sit under YHVH's inYHVH's. Salvation was only given to humanity and not offered to any other being. The Lamb was slain before the foundation to provide an avenue for Christ to have an entry into the world. YHVH wanted a record of Himself deposited into creation, to be the blueprint for the formation and foundation of Himself within humanity. This is His DNA, through Christ, being left on the face of the earth so that we can become sons bearing His image. That is why He went to the cross and rose again - to leave us a record, through communion, to have a blueprint for our future. If He had not gone there, we would have never had the record of victory here.

"...The mountain of the Lord shall be established in the top of the mountains..." (Isaiah 2:2KJV). The Throne of God is seated on a mountain. The mountain is the House of God. Everything that is the functionality of the Throne, upon the top of it, is at work in the government of the house that sits underneath it. All the chambers that relate to the government of the throne sit in the mountain of God. That is why the Bible says, *"Who may ascend into the hill of the LORD... he who has clean hands and a pure heart"* (Psalm 24:3-4 NKJV, emphasis mine). It does not say up the outside of the hill or mountain, but into. The Bible says, *"Jesus went up into a mountain apart to pray"* (Matthew 14:23 KJV). He did not climb the outside of the mountain. He went up and into the mountain of the government of Heaven. While He was in the middle of the government of Heaven, in the courts of YHVH, He prayed. It is because your position in the mountain of God establishes the government of YHVH on the earth through you. This positioning is vital for a perspective and view from Heaven to earth, not earth to Heaven. Christ, to me, means the realm of the government of the anointing He walks in. Our walk is about this realm.

It is written that our body is the temple of the Holy Spirit: *"Or don't you know that your body is a temple of the Ruach* ha-Kodesh who is in you, whom you have from God, and that you are not your own?" (1 Corinthians 6:19 TLV). You and I are revealed as the temple of the Holy Spirit. We are the house of the resident presence of YHVH. Therefore, we are also revealed as the mountain of YHVH. We become a blueprint on earth of what is in Heaven. If we are mountains, then on the top of each of our mountains, there is a throne that sits in the same way, as it is in Heaven with YHVH's throne. This will be displayed down here in the same way. That is why the Bible says, *"...The mountain of the Lord's house shall be established in the top of the mountains..."* (Isaiah 2:2 KJV).

What YHVH is revealing about the mountains comes out of the government of the Seat of Rest. The Seat of Rest is an internal throne that empowers the external position of your throne, on your mountain. Without the functioning of the Seat of Rest, you will not be able to properly assume the throne of your mountain seat. It is from the Seat of Rest that we rule over our bodies and the environment around us, giving us domain to influence our environment. It is on the Seat of Rest that we learn how to surrender while we are being trained, equipped, and repositioned into lordship. Before we can rule, we must have Him sitting on the seat that is on our mountain. The key I have found was me abdicating that throne on my mountain and positioning YHSVH there in the very early stages of my walk in YHVH. It is here that we learn to submit to His Lordship. When we learn how to submit, we are trained in how to become a lord ourselves. Through this, we learn how to rule ourselves and become a king. YHSVH is known as the *"Lord of lords and King of kings"* (Revelation 17:14 NKJV).

> *"For He received from God the Father honour and glory, when there came such a voice to him from the excellent glory, This is my beloved Son, in whom I am well pleased. And this voice which came from heaven we heard, when we were with him in the holy mount. We have also a more sure word of prophecy; whereunto ye do well that ye take heed, as unto a light that shineth in a dark place, until the day dawn, and the day star arise in your hearts."* (2 Peter 1:17–19 KJV)

The government is all about what goes on in the mountain. It is where the glory is going to be revealed from, within the mountain. Whatever happens on the outside of the mountain is going to be a reflection of what goes on in it. It is what goes on in our life that is going to be displayed around our life. YHVH wants us to be free. He wants us to come into lordship and surrender to His government.

Before we can rule and dispossess what is on the mountains, in the realm of the kingdom that is in corruption, we have to learn to rule on our mountains and dispossess the power that corruption has had over our life.

"...*Be imitators of God...*" (Ephesians 5:1 NKJV). YHVH's desire is to teach us to rule through our spirit man, into our soul, through our body, and into the world around us. We are a spirit being, that has a soul, who lives in a physical body. The spirit of the presence of YHVH will change our spirit, transform our soul, and transfigure our bodies. We must learn to be imitators of YHVH. If He rules from a Throne, then we need to learn to rule from a throne.

So what is the Seat of Rest? The Seat of Rest is our alignment into the desire of the Father. It is our engagement into the purpose of YHVH and our desire coming to fruition in the world around us. It is us setting ourselves apart to yield to Him and surrender to His government in our life. This internally equips us to engage the external, to change those things in the external, so they take on the reflection of the internal. We are going to terraform the face of the earth. When we carry that reflection inside of us, with the harmony of heaven, we are going to walk into everything that is chaos and bring divine order.

The earth's appearance is going to begin to change. That is why it is groaning for our manifestation. We practice on the earth, so that when we are in the galaxies, we can change them as well, because that is what they are waiting for. They are waiting for us to show up. The Bible says, "*For the creation eagerly awaits the revelation of the sons of God*" (Romans 8:19 TLV).

It is longing for us to take our place; but we cannot take our place there, unless we take our place here first. YHVH wants this temple sorted out and in the right order. The key principle is to experience life from the arena and aspect of the Father, and use life's circumstances to train, enable, and empower us to change every influence of all that is around our lives.

As a ruler on a mountain, there will be consequences to sin. When we have responsibility, there are always consequences for things we do that are not right. Even if we do them in the dark, where we think no one can see or be affected by our sin, there are consequences to positional power. There are always consequences to our actions, good and bad. One of the key things we need to understand is that there is a Great Cloud of Witnesses who are around us, watching us every day of our life. They do not have a reference for our sin, because no sin can be in the realm of the heavens. They are just waiting for us to get our act together. Whatever we are doing, they are all watching. Our brain and the nature of our sin do not want us to look and think of this perspective, because knowing we are never alone, begins to bring positive peer pressure on our life to change. Even what we consider to be the smallest things, can still spoil the vine. When we do not do right in them, it is as if we tie a rag around a fox's tail and light it.

> *"So Samson went and caught 300 foxes, and took torches, turned the foxes tail to tail and put one torch between every two tails. Then he set fire to the torches and released them into the standing grain of the Philistines, Thus he burned up both the stacks and the standing grain, along with vineyards and olive trees."* (Judges 15:4-5 TLV)

The motivation of the government of our heart is important in order to engage the Kingdom realm. We are going to find the Seat of Rest through surrender to Lordship. If we have never done that verbally, we can do it together now. I have found that ninety-five percent of Christians have never abdicated the throne of their heart, stepped off it, nor asked YHSVH to come and be seated as Lord and King of their heart and life. Find a place where you can take a step forward, pray this prayer, then confess with your mouth and speak the things that I have written.

"Father, today I want to thank You for making a way for me to come before Your presence. Lord, today, by faith, I step into the realm of Your presence."

ACTIVATION

Father, today while I am in this realm of Your presence, forgive me for not surrendering to the absolute government of Your Kingdom in my life. Right now, YHSVH, I willfully and with desire abdicate the throne of my heart so that You will come and seat Yourself as Lord and as King – as Lord of lords and King of kings, over my life. I surrender my mountain, its domain, and its government into Your Hands. I give You the keys of my heart. I give You the keys to every doorway of my spirit, soul, and body. Today, YHSVH, I thank You, that by faith, You are now seated on the throne of my life as Lord. Train me to surrender to Your Lordship. In that place of maturity, teach me to know how to assume responsibility for the seat of government in my life. Now, Lord, I step back into the atmosphere of earth, and I bring You into this realm. Teach me how to administrate this in YHSVH's Name.

CHAPTER 7

THE FUNCTION OF WISDOM

The Seven Spirits of God form the Menorah candlestick with the Spirit of the Lord at the centre of it all. The Spirit of the Lord, being the centre of the seven, does not appear as distinctively masculine or feminine. The Spirit of Wisdom is one of the Seven Spirits of God: three of them are feminine in their nature and appearance while the other three are masculine. The Seven Spirits of God authorise us in our position on earth. They mandate, equip, and set us in place. They are our tutors according to Galatians 4:1–2. *"Now I say that the heir, as long as he is a child, does not differ at all from a slave, though he is master of all, but is under guardians and stewards until the time appointed by the father."*

I have spent a lot of time with the Spirit of Wisdom because I have had to learn about the Father's house and about the way Wisdom functioned at the very beginning. In this chapter I am going to teach about the function of Wisdom and what she looks like when she is operating in and around the life of a person.

Here is Wisdom, introducing herself to us:

"In the beginning I was there,
for God possessed me even before he created the universe.
From eternity past I was set in place,
before the world began" (Proverbs 8:22-23 TPT)

She was one of the first sentient beings created by the Father, Son and Holy Spirit. There was also an angelic sentient being created to be with the Spirit of Wisdom, found in the book of Proverbs, called Prudence, *"I wisdom dwell with prudence, and find out knowledge and discretion"* (Proverbs 8:12 KJ2000).

It is important to understand the Spirit of Wisdom and her function because of the increasing awareness of the knowledge of trading floors, and what is coming to the world as a result. There are things that have been prophesied and spoken out that we know are coming because they are in scripture. Creation has been waiting and looking expectantly to this time for the last thirty or forty years as this increasing knowledge of the functionality of the trading floors has been released. YHVH has appointed men and women over the earth to re-set it to His original design. It is not going to be the people who we would normally expect who will be doing this, or who may have world-wide ministries. When His government is revealed in this way, you will find many of those people will have been hidden and not necessarily known by anyone. Men and women who have been trained by YHVH in secret will be doing really unusual things on the face of the earth.

It is all about the function and role and the participation of the Spirit of Wisdom in these activities. She will be delivering the treasuries of Heaven that Solomon had in his day back to the earth. They are coming to the sons of YHVH out of the storehouse of Melchizedek. The Spirit of Wisdom is functioning in her role. The last time she visited the earth like this was in Solomon's day. She has waited for our day, for us to be in a position and to be trained and equipped to where she can deliver to the sons that which is needful out of Heaven, so that the sons can function and participate to be able to be displayed as kings on the earth.

There is a lot that is about to change on the face of the earth in the coming ages. Some of it is going to shock people and scare them because of the way it is going to be revealed, unless they have insight and understanding about what the Spirit of Wisdom is doing and what is going on. Nations are going to shake because kings who have understanding and knowledge and relational connection to the Spirit of Wisdom are going to arise. They will be positioned in such a way to be able to dictate how things are going to be done on the earth. They will frame it out of Heaven and be able to breathe into this reality from their position and their throne in Heaven the same way Solomon did. This is the government that YHVH is looking to bring into place on the face of the earth. It is a hidden government like a vizier to a king. He is delivering viziers to the earth to be next to the King of Kings to hear His counsel and to administrate Heaven on the earth. I am really excited about the unveiling of our future in the roles that many of us will be able to participate in. I stand here today as a son telling you that He is preparing to reveal much of what we have dreamed about in these areas to the earth.

> *"My son, keep my words, And treasure my commands within you. Keep my commands and live, And my law as the apple of your eye. Bind them on your fingers; Write them on the tablet of your heart. Say to wisdom, 'You are my sister,' And call understanding your nearest kin..."* (Proverbs 7:1–4 NKJV)

> *"Does not wisdom cry out, and understanding lift up her voice..."* (Proverbs 8:1)

We see in the verses above that the Spirit of Understanding and the Spirit of Wisdom are feminine.

"That they may keep you from the immoral woman, From the seductress who flatters with her words. For at the window of my house I looked through my lattice, And saw among the simple, I perceived among the youths, A young man devoid of understanding." (Proverbs 7:5–7 NKJV)

Solomon is talking about finances and money along with how a person will sometimes go after a harlot to get their heart's desire, instead of receiving from the Father so they can become self-sufficient. This is the fruit of someone who rescues himself. *"...And saw among the simple ..."* (Proverbs 7:7 NKJV) shows that YHVH considers people simple who chase these things.

"Immediately he went after her, as an ox goes to the slaughter, Or as a fool to the correction of the stocks, till an arrow struck his liver. As a bird hastens to the snare, He did not know it would cost his life." (Proverbs 7:22-23 NKJV)

It is interesting that the liver is associated with blood pressure and the cleansing of the blood. Often a person who struggles financially also struggles with blood issues and/or their families may have trouble along these lines. Many businessmen who suffer from high blood pressure and heart conditions have struggled financially where hope has been deferred on a continual basis. This I believe is directly related to the above issues. There is someone who watches over the area of finances, and her name is Wisdom.

"Does not wisdom cry out, and understanding lift up her voice? She takes her stand on the top of the high hill, beside the way, where the paths meet. She cries out by the gates, at the entry of the city, at the entrance of the doors.... 'Wickedness is an abomination to my lips. All the words of my mouth are with righteousness; nothing crooked or perverse is in them. They are all plain to him who understands, and right to those who find knowledge... I, wisdom, dwell with prudence and find out knowledge and discretion. The fear of the Lord is to hate evil; Pride and arrogance and the evil way and the perverse mouth I hate. Counsel is mine, and sound wisdom; I am understanding, I have strength. By me kings reign, and rulers decree justice. By me princes rule, and nobles, all the judges of the earth. I love those who love me, and those who seek me diligently will find

> me. Riches and honor are with me, Enduring riches and right-
> eousness."' (Proverbs 8:1–3, 7–9, 12–18 NKJV)

The Spirit of Wisdom is talking about herself here: she says, "My kings reign and my princes decree." Unless you have built a purposeful relationship with the Spirit of Wisdom and been mentored and trained by her, and spent time around her, you will not be able to be displayed in full measure as a king, prince or lord.

> *"My fruit is better than gold, yes, than fine gold, And my rev-*
> *enue than choice silver. I traverse the way of righteousness, In*
> *the midst of the paths of justice, That I may cause those who*
> *love me to inherit wealth, That I may fill their treasuries. 'The*
> *Lord possessed me at the beginning of His way, Before His*
> *works of old.'"* (Proverbs 8:19–22 NKJV)

This scripture is referring to creation. YHVH possessed Wisdom in this way.

> *"I have been established from everlasting, From the beginning,*
> *before there was ever an earth. When there were no depths I*
> *was brought forth, When there were no fountains abounding*
> *with water. Before the mountains were settled, Before the hills,*
> *I was brought forth; While as yet He had not made the earth or*
> *the fields, Or the primal dust of the world."* (Proverbs 8:23,28
> NKJV)

That dust is monatomic – the primal dust of the world.

> "When He prepared the heavens, I was there, When He drew a
> circle on the face" *[which are the four corners]* "of the deep,
> When He established the clouds above" *[which is the rulership*
> *of the sons],* "When He strengthened the fountains of the
> deep" [which is the glory in the earth], *"When He assigned to the*
> *sea its limit, So that the waters would not transgress His com-*
> *mand, When He marked out the foundations of the earth, Then*
> *I was beside Him as a master craftsman; And I was daily His*
> *delight, Rejoicing always before Him, Rejoicing in His inhabit-*
> *ed world, And my delight was with the sons of men."* (Proverbs
> 8:27,31 NKJV)

The Spirit of Wisdom is a key of David, as is rejoicing.

"...Now therefore listen to me, my children, For blessed are those who keep my ways..." (Proverb 8:32 NKJV)

"Keep my way" should make us think of paths and ancient ways.

> *"Now therefore, listen to me, my children, For blessed are those who keep my ways. Hear instruction and be wise, And do not disdain it. Blessed is the man who listens to me, Watching daily at my gates, Waiting at the posts of my doors. For whoever finds me finds life, And obtains favor from the Lord; But he who sins against me wrongs his own soul; All those who hate me love death. Wisdom has built her house, She has hewn out her seven pillars; She has slaughtered her meat, She has mixed her wine, She has also furnished her table. She has sent out her maidens, She cries out from the highest places of the city, 'Whoever is simple, let him turn in here!' As for him who lacks understanding, she says to him, 'Come, eat of my bread And drink of the wine I have mixed. Forsake foolishness and live, And go in the way of understanding.' He who corrects a scoffer gets shame for himself, And he who rebukes a wicked man only harms himself. Do not correct a scoffer, lest he hate you; Rebuke a wise man, and he will love you. Give instruction to a wise man, and he will be still wiser; Teach a just man, and he will increase in learning. 'The fear of the Lord is the beginning of wisdom, And the knowledge of the Holy One is understanding. For by me your days will be multiplied, And years of life will be added to you.'"* (Proverbs 8:31-9:11 NKJV)

The passages you've read show the book of Proverbs is full of the Spirit of Wisdom trying to communicate with humanity. It shows a multidimensional being's desire to have mankind – who is a two, three, or four dimensional being – understand that she has a way that leads and keeps us in the path of life.

Wisdom is an amazing being. She stands about eight feet high. She has long hair down to her waist, and it often blowing in the wind of YHVH. Her garment is like translucent blue-purple with gold woven into it and a golden sash. Within the sash it appears multi-dimensional and has galaxies within it. She has a golden sceptre in her right hand, which displays her as a queen within heavenly realms. The Spirit of Wisdom is actually a true queen in Heaven, unlike the mother figure of Mary. She holds inside her hand a massive golden sceptre.

When she hits the earth, the earth trembles similarly to the way it shakes when the voice of YHVH is released into creation. He is with her because she has been with Him and knows the Father from the beginning of His ways. A crown sits on her head, and sometimes her eyes are like fire that burns with a passion for the sons of YHVH to come into fruitfulness. When she speaks, it is like thunder, yet like a whisper of silk. She is an amazing being.

"Through wisdom a house is built, And by understanding it is established; By knowledge the rooms are filled With all precious and pleasant riches" (Proverbs 24:3–4 NKJV). I do not know about you, but to me that sounds like *"good measure, pressed down, shaken together, and running over will be put into your bosom"* (Luke 6:38 NKJV), with nowhere to put any more.

What is Wisdom?

Wisdom is knowing what to do, when to do it, and how to do it. Have you ever been in a circumstance where you just happen to be in the right place at the right time? The circumstances are perfect for you to connect with the right person, to do the right thing, at the right time, and then suddenly you find that your treasures are running over. Have you ever been in that situation? If you have not, then you have not been around the Spirit of Wisdom. She will orchestrate those things to happen around you. "I just happened to meet someone and we happened to be talking about something, and I just happened to know someone that could actually just help you with that thing you have wanted to do for the last ten years..." That is the Spirit of Wisdom. Where there is a list of "happened-to's", weird happenings, and circumstances where "it just happened to just happen," that is the Spirit of Wisdom functioning around you. She is interested in you. When the Spirit of Wisdom comes around, things you have been trying to do for years are just done. This is how she works. It is as if you are going one way one day, the next day you are going a completely different way, and you wonder, "How did that happen?"

When the Spirit of Wisdom is involved in what you are doing, her desire is to watch what you are doing and then bring affirmation by being involved in a personal way. She affirms her involvement as she watches over what you are doing. I have noticed that whatever she looks at and whatever catches her attention seems to work out and come to pass. The Father so trusts her because she was with Him in the beginning of His ways before the framework of creation in any way was put in place.

Wisdom is having YHVH's perspective on any situation, so we can make a sound decision in every circumstance and unfold the perfect will of YHVH. He is building a great corporate body of sons who are going to make an impact within creation and the human race as a species. For us to be able to function like this, we need Wisdom in every area of function we participate with. This body of sons to me is not necessarily a building. This has the capacity to be a group made from a person in Australia, someone in New Zealand, someone else in America, another in Ireland, someone in England, Scotland, Singapore, Switzerland, Holland, Italy, Canada, Germany or anywhere else, all getting together at the same time, in the same place, in the council of YHVH. All are together looking at what YHVH is doing. It is a union of common desire. It is an establishing of a body of people with a common desire to find the heart of YHVH. Out of that place, there is an unfolding and revealing through Wisdom which impacts creation. It is not about us as individuals coming to meet our own needs. In one nation, a study was done in which the following question was asked of a large number of people: "Why is the church here?" A very high percentage of them said, "To meet my needs." I am sorry. I have got some bad news for you: that is not why the house of YHVH exists.

In my opinion, a church "building" is not a place to just gather in together. The function of a building in theory should be to house a gate into the realm of Heaven for the body to be able to ascend into YHVH's presence and to descend again to bring life to the earth. *"For the bread of God is He who comes down from heaven and gives life to the world"* (John 6:33 NKJV). But unfortunately, that is not necessarily what I see happening in most church buildings. To most, going to church is primarily about getting filled for the week. I have noticed that many only come to receive from a church and not to contribute what they should have received from their union with YHVH during the week to add in at the corporate level. Mostly it is because people either do not know how to engage or ascend into His presence or have been lazy in their pursuit of YHVH during the week. Do I love His body? Yes: I served in one body for twenty-eight years. I have witnessed this behaviour of people in this system over these years. But when Wisdom comes, we can see the desire she has for us to know the Fear of the Lord.

> *"Wisdom is the principal thing; therefore get wisdom: and with all your getting get understanding. Exalt her, and she shall promote you..."* (Proverbs 4:7–8 KJV 2000)

There are so many aspects about the Spirit of Wisdom in the book of Proverbs that talk about the function of wisdom. The whole book of Proverbs is Solomon trying to describe his relationship with the Spirit of Wisdom and what she did with him before he lost it. Much of what happened to Solomon was due directly to him trading with the king of Tyre and the prince of Tyris. This is a picture of Lucifer and what he did. It is a picture of his operation that has positioned him over finances and illegal trading in the earth and in the heavens. The actual king of Tyre had two daughters, Jezebel and Atheliah. One went after the control of finances and the other positioned herself to capture the heart of worship to be able to control all religious activities and is the spiritual head of any religious activity. This presented a picture of a false godhead made of the king of Tyre, Atheliah and Jezebel.

> *"Exalt her, and she shall promote you: she shall bring you to honor, when you do embrace her. She shall give to your head an ornament of grace: a crown of glory shall she deliver to you."* (Proverbs 4:8–9 KJV 2000)

I do not know about you, but when I read these scriptures, I feel like I have been short-sighted not to get to know the Spirit of Wisdom as a being in person sooner, especially as it has been over ten years since the Lord started speaking to me about the Spirit of Wisdom. I can remember when I first taught about the Seven Spirits of God. Some of the comments made at that stage felt like I was being stoned. One of the phrases I really like is described in this next statement: I started trouble on the face of the earth that day; but it was good trouble because YHVH wants to trouble your troubles, to really trouble the trouble that is troubling you, because that leads to repentance.

> *"Who is a wise man and endued with knowledge among you? Let him show out of a good life his works with meekness of wisdom. But if you have bitter envying and strife in your hearts, boast not, and lie not against the truth. This wisdom descends not from above, but is earthly, sensual, demonic. For where envying and strife is, there is confusion and every evil work. But the wisdom that is from above is first pure, then peaceable, gentle, and compliant, full of mercy and good fruits, without partiality, and without hypocrisy. And the fruit of righteousness is sown in peace by them that make peace."* (James 3:13–18 KJ2000)

The wisdom of the world gives success in life to a limited level but it lacks eternal and spiritual insight. The Holy Spirit gives wisdom beyond what the world can give. The Wisdom of the Lord changes how we view and live life from a completely different perspective and with different results.

> *"And God gave Solomon wisdom and exceedingly great understanding, and largeness of heart like the sand on the seashore. Thus Solomon's wisdom excelled the wisdom of all the men of*

the East and all the wisdom of Egypt. For he was wiser than all men..." (1 Kings 4:29,31 NKJV)

Solomon is the first man that displayed in full measure one of the Seven Spirits of YHVH's authorisation for full manifestation on earth.

Wisdom: The Foundation for Success

Your relationship with the Spirit of Wisdom is the first foundational requirement for success in your life. Do you realise that YHVH gives Wisdom to ungodly men because the body of Christ will often not receive her? Wisdom has to land somewhere on the earth but many in the body of Christ have been closed off to or in complete ignorance of who she is, and they have refused to receive the riches and overflow of abundance she brings. When Wisdom releases from Heaven what is necessary and it comes into creation, it must land somewhere. If the body of Christ does not receive it, then it will land on the heathen. Some people do not want to have anything to do with wealth and would rather remain in poverty as a concept of spirituality. Much of the reason the body of Christ does not have wealth at this point is because they have rejected the Spirit of Wisdom, who she is and her function. They generally have no knowledge of who she is due to the lack of teaching and engagement with her as a being. Often this is why unbelievers have the wealth on the face of the earth.

When YHVH came to visit the earth during the Industrial Revolution in the early 1600s, much in the way of finances changed hands. But the church was not involved in it because of their poverty mentality: they preferred to remain poor as a sign of spirituality. Through a vow of poverty made by many religious orders who led the people, the Spirit of Wisdom was rejected. Due to this, the provision at her disposal was also rejected. From my perspective, the body of Christ has lived under that vow of poverty and famine ever since. The Spirit of Wisdom is brooding over the face of the earth again to purposefully engage with those who will hear her, get understanding and prepare themselves in relationship with her.

> *"Wisdom is the principal thing; therefore get wisdom: and with all your getting get understanding Exalt her, and she shall promote you: she shall bring you to honor, when you do embrace her."* (Proverbs 4:7–8 KJ2000)

> *"Long life is in her right hand; In her left hand are riches and honor."* (Proverbs 3:16 AMP)

This is a key to the beginning of your engagement with the Spirit of Wisdom. There is action in these verses.

The first is calling us to exalt her. Exaltation is not worship. The dictionary gives the definition as follows:

exalt (verb): /ig'zôlt/

- think or speak very highly of (someone or something).
  "the party will continue to exalt their hero"

- raise to a higher rank or position.
  "this naturally exalts the peasant above his brethren in the same rank of society"

- make noble in character; dignify.
  "romanticism liberated the imagination and exalted the emotions"[13]

So, to exalt Wisdom means to give due honour to the source of the supply and to acknowledge the provision that she has brought to you from the hand of the Father.

The second action is for us to embrace her.

The first time I encountered the Spirit of Wisdom, it freaked me out. You have this ethereal, amazing being the Bible tells me to embrace and engage in relationship. One of the characteristics of the Spirit of Wisdom is that she is like a mother hen who broods over her chickens and overshadows them like a mother. If you do not embrace her purposefully, it is very difficult to acknowledge her. I do not go and worship the Spirit of

---

[13] *Google Dictionary,* s.v. "exalt."

Wisdom. She is a companion of the Lord given to deliver the treasures and provision of Heaven to the earth out of Melchizedek's treasure chamber.

Characteristics of Wisdom

Integrity

Let's discuss some of the characteristics of Wisdom. The first is integrity. Integrity means of sound moral character, wholesome and trustworthy. The trials we go through are a crucible. These trials help to develop and mould our character in the right way. In the middle of that crucible, you get understanding, which is wholesome and trustworthy. Many believers are not trustworthy. An example of this in its simplest form could be when a shopper receives five cents more from the teller than they should for change. Do they keep it or do they give it back? These small things reveal internal character that the Spirit of Wisdom is looking to be developed in our lives.

If you are a tradesman and you leave a mess in someone's house after you have done your work, you show yourself lacking excellence in all that you do because you should clean up after yourself. All these small things reveal your internal character traits. The Spirit of Wisdom looks for excellence because she is excellent in all her ways. Excellence is a character trait that will follow your relational connection to her. If you are in work that you do not like and you do not do a full day's work or leave five minutes early, you lack integrity and excellence. I have some unbelievers that work for me better than the sons of God.

These are some of the simple reasons the Spirit of Wisdom is not interested in the sons: though they are the ones who should be having the inheritance, their behaviour does not reveal her in what they do. She goes to those who are trustworthy, honourable and excellent in all that they do: unfortunately, many of them are unbelievers who function more highly than the sons do. If we are not responsible in the small things, we will never receive the big things we dream of. Often I find people like dreaming about one day when some big thing may happen, but they will not allow their character to be adjusted to walk with integrity. We have to get prepared for that big thing. If we are not prepared, the big thing is not going to happen.

> *"The fear of the LORD is the beginning of wisdom: and the knowledge of the Holy One is understanding. For by me your days shall be multiplied, and the years of your life shall be increased."* (Proverbs 9:10,11 KJ2000)

If you want to live a prosperous, long life and increase your days, get to know the Spirit of Wisdom. She is beautiful, and I think she is amazing.

Creativity

Creativity is another characteristic of Wisdom. Creativity refers to original, imaginative, progressive, new ideas, forms or ways of doing of familiar tasks that have not been seen before. One of the key expressions of the Spirit of Wisdom is creativity, not only in business but also in the arts. Many creative expressions are starting to be brought back into the church. All the expression of the different sciences are being returned because they are creative as well, and guess who sits over the top of creativity? The Spirit of Wisdom.

Prudence is an angel who dwells with the Spirit of Wisdom, and she wants to give creative ideas and witty inventions to the sons of God. Creative ideas are released into creation by Prudence, but because the sons are not in a place in their character, in their lifestyle or in understanding their position, they are unable to receive them. The heathen will often receive these ideas and will benefit from them because the sons have not been proven trustworthy and diligent in their pursuit of relationship and excellence.

"Then I was beside Him as a master craftsman; And I was daily His delight, Rejoicing always before Him, Rejoicing in His inhabited world, And my delight was with the sons of men." (Proverbs 8:30–31 NKJV)

The Spirit of Wisdom loves creativity to the max. She loves it when there is creativity in the body of Christ. She loves music, painting, flags and the expression of all the arts. She loves the chaos of creativity – to her, it is divine order. That is why when we all sing in the spirit it has the appearance of chaos, but to her it is divine order.

Excellence

The third characteristic of Wisdom is excellence. *"... An excellent spirit, knowledge, understanding, interpreting dreams, solving riddles, and explaining enigmas were found in this Daniel..."* (Daniel 5:12 NKJV).

There is a difference between doing things excellently with an excellent spirit and having a spirit of excellence which is a driving, destructive thing. A spirit of excellence drives perfection. When anything is out of order, perfection will manifest and rule with a rod of iron. You then come under an enslavement of bondage to the drive of the spirit of excellence, so that everything must look excellent in the appearance of perfection. But if you function with the Spirit of Wisdom, you will give the time to do whatever your call is without anyone having to tell you to do it. For example, simple things make a difference: if you see a bit of paper on the floor, you pick it up. Dust in the corner? You clean it without anyone looking. You see the lights need fixing? You fix them without anyone telling you to. That is the Spirit of Wisdom working within an individual's life.

When people put chewing gum under their seats instead of throwing it away properly, it reveals there is no desire for excellence in them. There is a difference between the religious spirit and a rebellious spirit regarding excellence. Often, a religious spirit requires actions that are confined to activities without the connection to the presence of God, but requires and demands servitude through structures of laws. This is a way to try to create excellence. A person who rebels against the confinements of a religious spirit is often accused of having a rebellious spirit. That is not excellence. Excellence says, "I love YHVH and His presence. I am going to make the presentation of His house a place of joy and abundance for the glory of God to sit in.

When excellence is achieved voluntarily, it becomes a welcoming place for the Spirit of Wisdom to walk amongst her people and bless them and endow them with treasures from Heaven to fill the treasuries of the house of the Lord.

Excellence means excelling above others in your field and having superior quality, it does not mean being superior. It means giving attention to the most minute detail and taking care of all those things. It is the little things that are important to the Father, which brings an awareness of the awe of YHVH and the presentation of who He is to the community.

> *"As for these four young men, God gave them knowledge and skill in all literature and wisdom; and Daniel had understanding in all visions and dreams. Now at the end of the days, when the king had said that they should be brought in, the chief of the eunuchs brought them in before Nebuchadnezzar. Then the king interviewed them, and among them all none was found like Daniel, Hananiah, Mishael, and Azariah; therefore they served before the king. And in all matters of wisdom and understanding about which the king examined them, he found them ten times better than all the magicians and astrologers who were in all his realm. Thus Daniel continued until the first year of King Cyrus."* (Daniel 1:17–21 NKJV)

The Lord gave them supernatural knowledge and abilities without the necessity to go through a school of learning. The Word says YHVH gave it to them. When the Spirit of Wisdom is involved within your life and in an environment where excellence is displayed, you will be given access to revelatory abilities and understanding as a gift from Yahweh. This comes through the Spirit of Wisdom from the storehouse of knowledge and understanding of all things. Often this releases knowledge on being able to do things without knowing how you got there. When the Spirit of Wisdom is involved in all of our doings in life, she brings understanding into every sphere and operation of our daily life.

Ability to Interpret Dreams and Visions

Daniel did not have to be taught dream interpretation. Interestingly, he did not even have to hear from the king his dream. He was able to give the king what the king dreamed about and its interpretation without ever having to hear what the king's dream was. This is true dream interpretation that displayed the wisdom of Daniel. This displays the Spirit of Wisdom working through a man. The key to unlocking dream interpretation is not having knowledge from a natural realm of what everyone else believes. Imagery is but an act of entangling with YHVH that unlocks wisdom about the unknown. It is helpful to desire an active engagement with the Spirit of Wisdom and receive empowerment and knowledge to understand dreams and visions.

True wisdom originates from YHVH Himself and will often be revealed through the Spirit of Wisdom and her connection and involvement with humanity.

Examples of Wisdom

Let's look at some examples of Wisdom.

Joseph

The first is Joseph. Joseph had wisdom, understanding and the ability to see into the future. These empowered him to be able to plan and bring the knowledge of Heaven to bear on the earth to the point that he was able to prepare Egypt to become the centre of provision, literally having the ability to aid the whole earth in the days of famine.

"Then Pharaoh said to Joseph, 'Inasmuch as God has shown you all this, there is no one as discerning and wise as you. You shall be over my house, and all my people shall be ruled according to your word; only in regard to the throne will I be greater than you.' And Pharaoh said to Joseph, 'See, I have set you over all the land of Egypt'." (Genesis 41:39–41 NKJV)

Joseph was prepared through his trials in previous years. They created the ability in him and the platform to be able to handle the responsibility of being fully revealed within creation. Preparation time is important because it helps you deal with being completely hidden, which prepares you to be fully revealed. He was thrown in the lion's den, sold into slavery, accused of rape, put inside a jail, persecuted in jail and forgotten. But everywhere Joseph went, through serving and making his abilities available, he always ended up being put into leadership. This displays what the Spirit of Wisdom does within a person's environment – she will always display you and position you for leadership. When the Spirit of Wisdom is working with you in these arenas, one of the keys is to keep your heart with all diligence, for out of it flows the wellsprings of life.

Bezalel

Another person of wisdom was Bezalel. Wisdom's creative ability and skill in artistic design in golden jewellery can be found in Exodus 31:1.

"And the LORD spoke unto Moses, saying, See, I have called by name Bezalel the son of Uri, the son of Hur, of the tribe of Judah: And I have filled him with the spirit of God, in wisdom, and in understanding, and in knowledge, and in all manner of workmanship, To devise artistic works, to work in gold, and in silver, and in bronze, And in cutting of stones, to set them, and in carving of timber, to work in all manner of workmanship. And I, behold, I have given with him Oholiab, the son of Ahisamach, of the tribe of Dan: and in the hearts of all that are wise hearted I have put wisdom, that they may make all that I have commanded you." (Exodus 31:1 KJ2000)

When wisdom is released from Heaven, it unlocks and gives you the capacity to be able to do what is necessary for the Father to accomplish what He needs to get done. Can you imagine getting all understanding in workmanship of gold, silver, bronze and carving? Do you know how many years it takes to become a master craftsman? She is amazing.

Solomon

Solomon was given wisdom, creative ability and skill in government, architecture, art and science. You want to get a high IQ? Engage in relationship with the Spirit of Wisdom. She will give you the ability to accomplish what is necessary in your role in creation. Often this comes through activation of parts of your brain that you currently do not use. The major part of our brain that is inactive can begin to get activated when influenced by the Spirit of Wisdom. All that resides in Heaven can be unlocked within you as an endowment from the Father, when it is activated by the Spirit of Wisdom.

> *"Give therefore your servant an understanding heart to judge your people, that I may discern between good and bad: for who is able to judge this your so great a people? And the speech pleased the Lord, that Solomon had asked this thing."* (1 Kings 3:9–10 KJ2000)

I have spent the last three to four years praying, "Father I yield to the instruction of the Spirit of Wisdom for crafty, ingenious speech to be able to teach your people about the structure and the protocol of Heaven so they can enter the gates of the Glory of the Lord." I purposefully engage with the Spirit of Wisdom to hear her instruction as a tutor of my life to bring me to maturity as a son of God to be able to display the wisdom of YHVH in creation.

> *"And God said unto him, Because you have asked this thing, and have not asked for yourself long life; neither have asked riches for yourself, nor have asked the life of your enemies; but have asked for yourself understanding to discern justice; Behold, I have done according to your words: lo, I have given you a wise and an understanding heart; so that there was none like you before you, neither after you shall any arise like unto you.*

And I have also given you that which you have not asked, both riches, and honor: so that there shall not be any among the kings like unto you all your days. And if you will walk in my ways, to keep my statutes and my commandments, as your father David did walk, then I will lengthen your days." (1 Kings 3:11–13 KJ2000)

Remember, the Spirit of Wisdom will increase your days if you ask for the right thing. *"You ask and do not receive, because you ask amiss... "* (James 4:3 NKJV). I prayed for a wise and understanding heart that would carry the record of the Father's DNA inside of me for about a year, thanking the Father all the while. I prayed I would become a reflection of the platform of the Kingdom so that others can stand on it and engage the Kingdom realm of Heaven. When I was first learning I would embrace the Spirit of Wisdom, engage with her and allow my heart to reach out to be tutored in how to have an understanding heart. Often I found that I would need to do this repetitively to develop a relationship where I could be corrected and schooled in the function of having an understanding heart. This cannot be done outside of a relationship with the Spirit of Wisdom. She is not our mother and is not called a mother, she is called the Spirit of Wisdom and her delight is in the sons of men. She has delighted in the sons since before the creation of the earth: *"Then I was beside Him as a master craftsman; And I was daily His delight, Rejoicing always before Him, Rejoicing in His inhabited world, And my delight was with the sons of men"* (Proverbs 8:30–31 NKJV). She delights very much in our pursuit of rekindling our relationship with her.

Daniel

YHVH gave Daniel wisdom and creative ability in management, literature, and all spiritual matters. We can ask Spirit of Wisdom for ability in creativity, government and all spiritual matters.

"I have even heard of you, that the spirit of the gods is in you, and that light and understanding and excellent wisdom are found in you." (Daniel 5:14 KJV 2000)

Light, understanding and excellent wisdom: these three are the expression of the Beit Din (the bench of three). That is an expression of the oversight of the government of the Spirit of Wisdom over your life. One of the expressions of the revealing of the Spirit of Wisdom is the knowledge of the function of light. It is one of the reasons that I set about teaching on light. Understanding is not just having knowledge, but is an expression of life experience that has gone through discipline, that brings with it wisdom. Understanding is having an inner ability to also have knowledge and the ability to express it without it being learned. Excellent wisdom surpasses all the knowledge of humanity and releases the wisdom of YHVH into every environment and circumstance that empowers us to overcome and have answers for difficult things that we do not know about.

YHSVH

YHSVH's wisdom manifested itself in many different ways. One of them was the way that He had the capacity and the creative ability to touch the hearts of people and meet them at their point of need. This is the divine expression of the Spirit of Wisdom being revealed through His daily conversation with people.

As an example, consider the Samaritan woman who meets YHSVH at the well. She is taken by surprise when He asks her to give Him a drink. He knows her need is greater than a physical need for water. He draws her in to conversation when He says,

"Whoever drinks of this water will thirst again, but whoever drinks of the water that I shall give him will never thirst. But the water that I shall give him will become in him a fountain of water springing up into everlasting life." (John 4:13-14 NKJV)

Her reply?

"Sir, give me this water, that I may not thirst, nor come here to draw." (v. 15)

YSHVH tells her to call her husband, to which she replies she has none. YSHVH then reveals she has indeed had five husbands, and the one now is not married to her. *"Sir, I perceive you are a prophet,"* replies the woman (v. 19).

Wisdom is displaying who you are, being present in your character and integrity in what others are seeing through your life. An expression of wisdom in our personal life is having the ability to add into the mix answers that have pinpoint accuracy. This often creates an interest of others in conversation when they see this type of thing happening, and YHSVH displayed this all the time.

The Impact of Wisdom's Presence

If the Spirit of Wisdom is actively engaged in and around you, and you have an heart open to her, she will get drawn to observe you and be with you as you express this life to those around you. She will delight in administrating excellent wisdom through your life. She will whisper her secrets into your ear about finances and things that you do not know anything about.

"Both riches and honor come from You, And You reign over all. In Your hand is power and might; In Your hand it is to make great and to give strength to all" (1 Chronicles 29:12 NKJV). The verse says, "Both riches and honour". In Proverbs 8:18, the Spirit of Wisdom reveals *"Riches and honor are with me, Enduring riches and righteousness"* (NKJV). *Riches* does not mean a small amount. It is an overflowing, endless river that never runs dry in all aspects of life. Riches do not apologise for having too much, nor does it say that it cannot have any more. It creates the capacity to work with abundance to serve the needs of YHVH in creation. You have to learn how to handle the little things that are supplied from Heaven to be

able to handle the gold bars. Honour the small things so YHVH can give you the bigger ones.

I go into the river in Eden wanting an object to trade. I prefer big stones. While in the river, I find the biggest one and take it. I find as many big square diamonds as I can and I put them into my belly, through into the treasury room of my mountain. I come out and I then go onto the sea of glass to trade: "Daddy, I give you the riches of Heaven. I trade with Your riches for love." The Father delights in our attempts in our childlike estate to learn how to trade with the treasures that He has given us along those that we have found and discovered that we come to trade with.

The greatest key in the way I approach Him in all this is that He loves me. The Bible says, *"The silver is mine and the gold is mine, says the Lord of hosts"* (Haggai 2:8 KJ2000). One of the key things is to continually rejoice, no matter what your estate is regarding finances and the treasure that YHVH gives to you and others. Do not get drowned under the weight of having too much. Learn how to handle the little things first. Can you imagine the gold dust some of you have seen floating around in the air become one kilogram gold bars floating around? You will have the authorities showing up asking questions about how the gold is appearing and what you are doing with it! I have no doubt that they would want it. Can you imagine if they took it away and some more appeared – what would happen?! It is Melchizedek who decides how to dispense and give the precious things from the storehouse of the treasury room of YHVH.

The Spirit of Wisdom advises: *"My son, keep my words, And treasure my commands within you. Keep my commands and live, And my law as the apple of your eye. Bind them on your fingers; Write them on the tablet of your heart"* (Proverbs 7:1–3 NKJV). She says, *"Listen, for I will speak of excellent things, And from the opening of my lips will come right things; For my mouth will speak truth..."* (Proverbs 8:6–7a), and *"Riches and honor are with me, Enduring riches and righteousness. My fruit is better than gold, yes, than fine gold, And my revenue than choice silver"* (Proverbs 8:18–19). If it's not clear already, we should listen because, as Wisdom says,

> *"Now therefore, listen to me, my children,*
> *For blessed are those who keep my ways.*
> *Hear instruction and be wise,*
> *And do not disdain it.*
> *Blessed is the man who listens to me,*
> *Watching daily at my gates,*
> *Waiting at the posts of my doors.*
> *For whoever finds me finds life,*
> *And obtains favor from the Lord."* (Proverbs 8:32–35 NKJV)

Finally, consider that the Spirit of Wisdom says *"For by me your days will be multiplied, and years of life will be added to you"* (Proverbs 9:11 NKJV). When we engage with the Spirit of Wisdom, and when we engage with the Lord, we can be assured we will be shown secrets of the Kingdom. As the Lord says, *"Call to Me, and I will answer you, and show you great and mighty things, which you did not know"* (Jeremiah 33:3 NKJV), and, *"I will give you the treasures of darkness And Hidden riches of secret places, That you may know that I, the LORD, Who call you by your name, Am the God of Israel"* (Isaiah 45:3 NKJV).

The Spirit of Wisdom will reveal insight about governmental circles, about things going on in secret, and often things going on in the lives of people you know. When you actively engage with her as a tutor, she will be drawn to you. Suddenly you will find yourself being involved in and doing significant things. When you are subject to the tutelage of the Spirit of Wisdom, it unlocks and releases to you the entitlement to the knowledge of every single educational tool that has ever been on the face of the earth. In an instant, she will endow you with all of that knowledge. This is one of the privileges of having her tutelage and a personal connection to this being as one of the Seven

Spirits of God. This sounds like a good educational tool and process to me.

Let's have a look at the impact of Wisdom when she is around us. Here is a key scripture:

> *"And when the queen of Sheba heard of the fame of Solomon, she came to test Solomon with hard questions at Jerusalem, with a very great company, and camels that bore spices, and gold in abundance, and precious stones: and when she had come to Solomon, she spoke with him of all that was in her heart. And Solomon answered her all her questions: and there was nothing hid from Solomon which he answered her not. And when the queen of Sheba had seen the wisdom of Solomon, and the house that he had built, And the food of his table, and the seating of his officials, and the attendance of his servants, and their apparel; his cupbearers also, and their apparel; and his entryway by which he went up into the house of the LORD; there was no more spirit in her. And she said to the king, It was a true report which I heard in my own land of your acts, and of your wisdom: However I believed not their words, until I came, and my eyes had seen it: and, behold, the one half of the greatness of your wisdom was not told me: for you exceed the fame that I heard. Happy are your men, and happy are these your servants, who stand continually before you, and hear your wisdom."* (2 Chronicles 9:1–7 KJ2000)

Have you ever been in a meeting where people were talking about things that you knew nothing about? Suddenly, somebody turns to you and asks you something that you know nothing about. You give them the appropriate answer that completely unlocks wisdom into that environment. Often I find myself amazed at my answers, asking the question, "Where on earth did that come from?!" When I was twenty-three I was in a meeting in which I was applying for a supervisory and management position that I should not have really received, but I had some experience in some of it. They asked me a question in the interview to see if I could tell them the chemical formula of sodium metabisulfite. I answered, "Na_2S_2O." They thanked me and I was completely shocked! In this same meeting, they asked me questions and I suddenly would know the answers, leaving me wondering where the answers were coming from! It was the Spirit of Wisdom whispering in my ear, giving me answers to things I knew nothing about.

Skill, wisdom and all understanding of all matters concerning science are in the Bible.

When the Queen of Sheba was meeting with Solomon, the Bible says *"there was no more spirit in her"* (1 Kings 10:5 KJV), which means she was breathless and had no cognisant ability to function properly in the physical environment. In other words she became like a dead man. In modern day terms, we would say she was slain in the spirit. When the Spirit of Wisdom comes around and you truly begin to display her nature in what you are doing, people will be drawn to the government of the Glory of God in the place that you stand and they may fall on the floor. It is not because you are so good. It only comes from the display of the goodness of YHVH, which is the Glory of God in the land of the living.

The world is going to start hearing about what the sons of God are doing in communities. Suddenly, there will be an endowment of riches that will come to the house as they impact and change the community. The leaders of the community are going to come to you and ask how they can help. I am aware of people and know them personally at this point in time who have local government falling over themselves to help them in their endeavours in the community. They are going to construct buildings and the government will pay for the buildings and the renovations, because of how they are impacting the community. That sounds to me like Wisdom expressing herself. Getting the world to pay for everything is a good idea, considering YHVH owns the cattle and the mountains and the hills: *"For all the animals of the forest are mine, and I own the cattle on a thousand hills"* (Psalm 50:10 NLT). When we sit in the right position and placement with the correct government of YHVH, this type of activity will become normal, as transference of wealth occurs.

When Wisdom is around, you will have so much that you will not know what to do with it all. You will have the house of YHVH's delight around you. You will have the right resonant frequency, so when you worship, there is a resident tone that vibrates inside the meeting. Listen, people will come into a house to serve the house when Wisdom is there just because they want to get in the house. The Bible says all the kings of the earth came to see Solomon. *"All the kings of the earth sought audience with Solomon to hear the wisdom God had put in his heart"* (2 Chronicles 9:23 NIV) . This will become our daily life as the Lord unfolds our future.

"Blessed be the LORD your God, who delighted in you ..." (1 Kings 10:9 NKJV).

It is going to be amazing when the world comes and has to say out of their mouth that we are blessed by YHVH, because there would be no other answer to what they see. Everyone in Solomon's house was happy serving. Everyone was joyful in what they were doing because they were so blessed, there was abundance to everyone.

> *"Blessed be the LORD your God, who delighted in you to set you on his throne, to be king for the LORD your God .... And she gave the king a hundred and twenty talents of gold, and spices in great abundance, and precious stones: neither were there any such spices as the queen of Sheba gave King Solomon."* (2 Chronicles 9:8–9 KJ2000)

King for the Lord your God – not king and lord. When you are king for the Lord your God, you are ruler over everything. If you think you are king and lord, you will not rule over any-thing. People will serve you out of constraint, not out of desire. This is the part that I really love: *"...she gave the king a hun-dred and twenty talents of gold."* That is over $118 billion dol-lars' worth of gold! Man, that will fill up a treasury alright. Part of the evidence of Wisdom's presence is a continuous overflow-ing and immeasurable abundance in every area. It is not only us being able to create abundance and materialise it, but the kings of the earth bring their wealth and lay it at our feet. This does not come from having good systems in place or from having good capacity. It comes as an expression as people are drawn to the wisdom being expressed through us.

"And she gave the king [...] spices in great abundance..." Spices in those days were very expensive. Some spices were worth more than gold. And here is the one I love: she also gave precious stones. Now let me tell you something, if an ungodly queen can give precious stones to a godly king, why are you worried about YHVH giving precious stones to His people?

ACTIVATION

Hallelujah, Father! We want to thank You that the Spirit of Wisdom was with You at the very beginning. Father, we want to thank You that she was Your daily delight. She was with You before the foundations of the heavens and before the earth was formed. Spirit of Wisdom, I want to thank you that your desire is to be amongst the children of the sons of the Father. Spirit of Wisdom, today we invite you and ask you to come and make this your dwelling place. May the tabernacling branch of your sceptre be passed over this house so that the garments you carry in the glory, that you bear from the Father be ours. We pray that you would grace us with the manifestation of who you are within the house, in our lives, in our circumstances and in every environment we walk in. Holy Spirit, thank You that You have made a way for the Spirit of Wisdom to come by, sealing us with Your presence and with that seal of approval. Holy Spirit, we want to thank You today that You came willingly to look and wait for this day. This is an amazing day, Lord, to be alive. You chose us to be here in this day when the fullness of the sons is coming to bear on the earth. Lord, let it be according to Your Word, according to the testimony of who You are in Heaven, Father, and who we are in You, in Heaven and on the earth.

We welcome the administration of the crown of the Spirit of Wisdom. We welcome her oil, Lord, that we would drink the wine of her presence that she has mingled in the path by the corner of the doorpost and the ancient paths. Lord, we welcome all that comes with her: the angels, chancellors, magistrates, Wisdom's handmaidens and the sons of God that walk with her and bear witness, Father, to what she has done in the earth. Thank you for that, Lord. In the name of YHSVH. Amen.

CHAPTER 8

THE JOURNEY INTO BUSINESS

I would like to start this chapter by establishing some things regarding business. I consider myself a businessman and not a full-time minister. I have a limited liability corporation, which is Son of Thunder, Ltd., and I am a business partner in Son of Thunder Publications, Ltd. as well as the Nest online school. I also have several other businesses and we are working toward starting some others, which I am excited about .

I would like to share with you some of the things that we have walked through. A number of them have been very beneficial in our lives, while others have not been so pleasant but were still great learning experiences. Throughout the course of my life, I have owned about nine different businesses. Some of them have been very successful, some of them not so successful, but I am still a businessman.

There are things that I dream of obtaining in business that are fantastic and would be an amazing journey, but I must learn to stick within the boundaries that YHVH has given me. However, I have to be very careful that business does not capture too much of my attention. I must stay focused on what YHVH has me doing on the world stage at this point in time. I consider myself to be going about the business of YHVH. I am not saying it is not good to be a pastor, or a full-time minister in a church. There are those who are called to do that, and I honour that calling. I am just glad that I do not hold that position right now. And because of that, I am free to do and say what YHVH calls me to, without the hindrances or restrictions of a society of people who might oppose what we are doing as sons of YHVH.

It is my experience that any successful business professional has had to be hidden for a season while they go through brokenness. Somewhere further along the line when our life comes into order, we are unveiled and revealed by YHVH within the business community. I have found this over and over again in my own personal life.

Some business ventures that my wife and I started were not a success, but in the middle of these being unsuccessful, YHVH became our success. YHVH has had to break into our lives and deal intrinsically with some of the things that were sitting within us. As we have embraced the journey with YHVH through this, it has created a way for us to be able to come to maturity so that we could handle every aspect of our personal and business life.

As we walk through our brokenness, we may experience the process of alternately being revealed and then being hidden, both personally and within our business arena. I often find that it is the broken parts of us that lay the platform for YHVH to build on. This is especially true if our responses have been correct in the middle of what we have been going through. If our responses have not been right, YHVH will very lovingly – not always nicely, but always lovingly – take us through the process over and over, until we learn and begin to get our responses right to His pruning and loving discipline of our lives.

While running our second business, my wife and I learned that we had not laid a proper foundation in our first business. This caused us to have to go through the process of being undone to deal with the need to have money again, so we could learn how to respond correctly. The need to have money is a driving force that gets us focused on what we are doing as our supply, not our trust in YHVH to bless the works of our hands in what we are doing. We recognised what YHVH was trying to do for us. And even though it was a difficult journey, I would not trade the brokenness and the struggle for anything because of what this process worked in us as we responded to it. I find that some people do not allow YHVH to deal with them in the middle of their struggle. If you allow YHVH to deal with you, He can lead you on into perfection and you will go from glory to glory instead of from struggle to struggle. If you do not allow the process to unfold, then you will go around and around the same mountain and get stuck in the birthing chamber.

I was not always a businessman, and in some of the chapters of this book, we will look at other things that can affect us. In this chapter, I want to talk about your heart's preoccupation and whether you have your business, or your business has you. What is your heart set on?

You must get hold of your business and sit over it. If you allow it to occupy you, you may well find your time slipping away and being eaten by unproductivity. You end up working more and more hours within your business environment, trying to do what you should be doing in a normal working week. I have found in my personal experience that whenever my businesses began to preoccupy me, I would spend increasingly more time working. I would not be getting any more done than I normally would have when I worked a forty-hour week. The time I invested would creep up to forty-five, then fifty hours a week because my business was occupying me instead of my occupying it. I started to change the way I worked so the business did not possess me. I recognised there were things that YHVH was trying to bring me through that would empower me as a person and as a businessman, so that I would learn how to sit on my business and occupy it instead of it sitting on me and occupying me.

In the Bible Christ says, *"Occupy till I come"* (Luke 19:13 KJ2000). I learned through the process of my own personal life that I have to occupy my business. I have to sit over the top of it and engage with it. I have to engage with the mountain of the business and the angelic realm connected to the scroll of the business. Just engaging with this process has helped me get hold of my business in the right way. I am going to take you through an activation at the end of this chapter that will hopefully be helpful for you. This will give you some idea of the things that I do while I am engaging both with my business mountain and the angelic realm connected with the actual business itself.

One of the key things that I have learned about business is that it is not just enough for me to pray about it, but rather I need to get in and host my business. Earlier in my life, my wife and I would pray about our business. When we prayed, nothing would actually change within the business, which was a great frustration to us and we wondered why it was like that. The reason it was like that was because we were praying, but not sitting on the mountain of the business and occupying it. Praying is great but occupying is the key. YHVH spoke to me very clearly and said, "You are praying about this, but not occupying it and administering legislation over it." This revelation changed so much of my business life. It is a process that we all have to go through and does not happen in a moment. YHVH pointed out what I needed to be doing. It took me about a year to undo my old patterns of thinking and establish new patterns of how to occupy my business in a different way. Legislation is not a series of tick boxes that we want to get done to become successful. Success comes out of legislation formed with relationship, out of brokenness, where YHVH has taken you on a journey to be able to take full responsibility through Him moulding your life. When you administrate legislation over your business it is not about demanding what you want, it is about finding the heart of what YHVH wants in the middle of what you are doing. Again I want to reiterate that everything is based around relationship, not a religious system of tick boxes. The key is to remember that when YHVH comes in He does not take your side, He takes over. Legislation comes through the union of submission to be given authority to carry the role of being able to govern the works of your hands correctly.

One of the things that happens when we occupy something is that we have to allow it to get positioned in our heart in the right way, but not allow it to possess us. We make a place for it, instead of it making a place for us. We do not fit into our business, our business fits into who we are and what we are doing.

Once it fits into us and we are able to overshadow it, through that overshadowing we can begin to engage with our business in the right way by sitting over it and viewing it through YHVH's world. When we learn how to govern it, YHVH can then position us to administrate the Kingdom through what we are doing within the business, instead of the business sitting on us and governing us. Then we are not sitting under the weight of the business, like trying to carry it as if on the point of a pyramid with the whole thing sitting over the top of you. Through governing my business correctly by administrating from above it, I have learned how to sit in the middle of it; to occupy it and have my spirit man expand and have influence by filling the mountain of my business with my presence. *"And he has given us his Spirit within us so that we can have the assurance that he lives in us and that we live in him"* (1 John 4:13 TPT). A key Kingdom principle here is that because I am in Him and He is in me, He governs my life to sit within me to expand Himself out through me. Therefore I treat my business life, mountain, and what I do in the same way. This helps me to govern what I am occupying in the right way.

If you see your business as a pyramid that is upside down, you are either sitting on top of it, in the middle of it or underneath it, bearing the weight of it. If you are underneath it, you will be trying to carry the whole thing with its weight sitting on top of you. This is not what YHVH wants for us. It is best to be seated on the top, function through the middle where you engage with it, to then rule your whole business. The most successful point is to be able to sit over the top of it and sit in the middle of it to occupy it. Do not sit underneath it with it on top of you. Eventually as you learn how to govern it and occupy it, YHVH will reposition you into the middle of it in a place of maturity where you will not have to sit on the top or be underneath it. For me, I sit over my business and govern it until I come to a place of maturity and Christ does not have to govern it but it is Christ in me who releases me to govern it in Him. Our job is to inherit everything, so He will train us to maturity and then give it to us. It is still under His government through our relational union with Him. *"...[I]t is your Father's good pleasure to give you the Kingdom"* (Luke 12:32 KJV).

I have learned to look at my business as a multifaceted dimensional arena. YHVH can move in any way to establish the pattern of the Kingdom and bring the Kingdom to the earth. When you are sitting in the centre, you can operate out of any one of the facets of your business. You are looking out into Heaven and into the earth. You are looking sideways through the business to see what is happening.

The position of occupation of the centre is very important for me. There are some things that I have found helpful in positioning myself, so I am not just sitting over my business trying to govern it all the time. Rather, I am actually sitting in the middle of it, legislating and operating within my business in all of its different dimensions. Then I am able to have complete functionality throughout all that is around me.

As the owner of a business that had employees, I chose to know every aspect of the business by working in every area of the business and knowing how every part functioned. This helped me to know what my employees should and should not be doing, based on my experience within the business. I also recognised that when someone was working for me within the business, I would receive the blessing of YHVH for the works of their hands. This is one of the reasons I encourage people to start up their own businesses so that YHVH can bless the works of their hands rather than your employer being blessed by the works of your hands.

When I go into a business, I want to know every single operational aspect or facet of that business so that I know what should be going on within it. When things are not happening the way they should, I then know what to do and how to respond.

Now I want to talk about some of the negative things that can stop you from sitting in the middle of your mountain and occupying your place in the business, in the presence of YHVH. There are a number of things that can happen to get your business out of your heart. There are also ways to get your business into your heart. This understanding comes from my own personal experience and walk through my business life. I did not have anyone to turn to for advice, so I had to walk it out myself.

There are many sources and facets of stress in a business. There are demands from staff, financial pressures, the stress in productivity and stress in people not delivering what they are supposed to, just to name a few. People will not always do the things you want them to do. A lot of them need supervision or empowerment within supervision. If a person is not empowered, they will remain like an unemployed person, a slave, or a servant, and not be an active member of your staff.

Empowering people is one of the keys to unlocking the hearts of people towards your business. Whenever I have looked for leadership qualities in someone that I wanted to fill positions in the different businesses I have had, I always looked for someone who was motivated. This was more important to me than having someone who understood everything. I wanted someone in whom I could see the right traits that enabled me to train them correctly and then empower them into a position of responsibility to engage with my business. This would lead them to become an occupier and a help within the business.

Stress will leave your business sitting over you and you may feel like your business rules your life. Stress takes your business out of your heart, so you are not embracing or occupying it, but it is occupying you. Stress dislodges your ability to govern your business. Conflict is another influence that will take a business out of your heart. Conflicts will come. Conflict happens everywhere in life. Sometimes YHVH will allow or orchestrate situations to mature His sons through conflict. Often conflict happens in leadership because YHVH will use those that are closest to you to sand the rough edges off you. Resolving conflict in a right way is one of the most important facets of coming to maturity. Conflict is born out of decisions that can either enhance relationship or begin to fracture it.

Solve Conflicts Instead of Trying to Govern Over Them from Inside

The Word says, *"As iron sharpens iron, so people can improve each other [sharpen their friends]"* (Proverbs 27:17 EXB).

Admittedly, your key staff are not necessarily friends you walk closely with – sometimes they are, sometimes they are not. But I have found that key staff are people too and they have their own brokenness they have to deal with. When they bring that with them to work, conflicts can arise. Try to solve those conflicts, instead of trying to govern the conflict from inside. (Building relationship in the right way is the key to establishing good staff in personal relationships.) People are humans and very often staff may not want to do what you want them to do. You try to tell them what you want them to do. Perhaps because you have not trained them properly, they may not understand what you expect of them. It might be that the position is beyond their ability to grasp. They may even have oppression sitting over them as if they are unable to comprehend it. Some people apparently have a cognition barrier around them that makes it seem as if they do not want to learn anything. This was one of the issues I dealt with in my business. When we had staff members who seemed slow to grasp things, I learned how to govern them and then be an encourager, not just a "criticiser".

In my businesses, I would systematically take the staff through a training process again and again. If they were not successful I would recognise that there was an inability in them to process properly, which meant that they could not go further in the business.

Another thing that creates negativity is financial pressure. There are so many who suffer from financial pressure in business, particularly when they start out in business and they are lacking practical experience.

I remember starting up a business. The first ten weeks were amazing, but then it began to go downhill, and soon, the business started ruling me. In the end, I was working eighteen hours a day to try and make it successful. The more I worked, the more it needed me. The more it needed me, the more I had to work until I realised that I was going to burn out if I kept doing it that way. I knew we had to change. That is what financial pressure creates when you allow it to rule you.

I have been part of what I call public face business where the public is your client. It is a great experience to have an insulated business where you do not have to deal with people and you can just deal with the practical aspects of your business. Dealing with the practical is easy, because it is obedient to do exactly what you want it to do. You can put your equipment down on a table and it will stay there; it will not move as it does not have its own brain to choose obedience or to choose to do what it wants to do. People create an environment around us which is good for us because it makes us realise who we are and how we need to govern. Otherwise it would put demands on you and would create an atmosphere around you where you feel like you have to fight to maintain your identity.

One of the things I have learned to do is not fight; instead, I have learned to find the place of rest. I have done other teachings on the mountain of rest and those are helpful for understanding this place.

When I am experiencing a difficult situation or when I am disquieted inside about what is going on, a key thing I have discovered to help me is using a phrase that my wife and I say often: "This, too, soon will pass."

I have found that phrase to be helpful to reset myself, recognising that it will not be like this forever. For example, when healthy and able-bodied people move into a new home and move their furniture around, they are sore in their body afterwards. The pain comes from lifting and positioning items because doing so is not part of their daily routine.

If you are not used to doing something, you will feel a certain amount of pain from the activity. In my own experience with pain, I have had to learn to say, "This, too, soon will pass". If you hurt a muscle, the initial thought is that you are going to have that specific pain forever. You may wonder if you will ever be free from it, as you are living with the pain every day. But very slowly you will find that it starts to resolve itself. The one thing that really helps me get myself engaged with YHVH again is looking at the situation and thinking, "This, too, soon will pass. It is not going to be like this forever". Embracing that statement has been very helpful for me.

Another danger in business is that it can undermine your priority that family should be first. Your family should be in the centre of your heart, and everything else should be connected on threads leading to your heart. If your family is not in the centre of your heart and your business is in that place instead, then having your business connected to your heart will actually possess your life. I have had to fight while doing business to maintain my connectivity with my family and make them a priority. Setting up the primary relationship with my wife and purposing to listen to her voice if she felt that my priority had shifted from her, was very helpful. I have found that for a lot of business people, their business is at the centre of their heart, which dislodges family connection. Without that primary source of emotional fulfillment from your family, your connection with them will begin to break. The family unit is the most important unit of all.

It amazes me that when you want something done, you give it to a person who is already busy, and they will get it done. I have noticed that if you give it to someone who is not doing anything, it never seems to get done. That is just the way it seems to work. When you are engaging business in the right way, you will appear to be a high achiever as you are getting a lot done. At the same time, it will seem that there is always more and more that needs to be done. Sometimes when it is like that for me, I have learned to do what I call take stock. I will look at everything that is going on and reassess what my priorities have been. If my family has not been my first priority, then I realign things so that they are. I determine how to shut down wrong priorities so that they do not control my time with my family.

Your business will not always be with you. Being a business person and owning a business does not mean that your business is going to endure. I have owned nine different businesses and I thought that each one was "it" and that I was going to have them forever. Let me assure you, they will not always be with you. But there is something that should and will be with you forever, and that is your family. If they are not, it may be that there are issues in you. Things may have happened in your past that caused you problems. Circumstances of your environment or upbringing might have been against you. I am not saying that you are evil or bad because things happened and your family has been dislodged from you. As a business person, I have to fight to keep my family in the centre of what I am doing, in particular by saying no to some things. If you are successful in your business and busy in church-life, demands can come on you from church-life, particularly because you are good at the task. When it becomes evident that you are good at getting things done there can be pressure from church-life also to demand more and more from you.

People will give you projects and they will ask you, "Can you do this?" If you are not secure in who you are, you will get your affirmation from pleasing people, and the things they are giving you to do will add another achievement to your life while you are accomplishing other people's projects. If your affirmation comes out of what you have accomplished, then the result is that you will say yes to another project and your family will be further distanced from you.

I have found my security in my relationship with YHVH. I do not need affirmation from others, and actually do not really care about their opinion regarding me. There was a time I did care about opinions until YHVH dealt with me. It took about three years to deal with the junk in me that it caused. At one stage, someone came to me and asked if I would like to do something. I looked at them straight in the face and said, "No." Their face was shocked, reflecting their thought of how could I say no. Well, it was easy – it was two letters: *n-o*. Their answer was them continuing to tell me how I needed to do something, and how it was all part of who I was. My response was, "What part of *n-o* don't you understand? Like no, I am not going to do it." I have had to fight to keep my family in the centre of what I am doing.

There are aspects of business that I have learned to always expect YHVH to challenge me in. YHVH is interested in developing our character. We may not be, but He is. He will orchestrate circumstances to force us to look at our character. It is important for me to be pliable in my character with regard to my business involvement. I spent a number of years trying some concepts in the last businesses that I have recently released. It was an amazing experience. I spent two or three years working with the staff to train them individually in what I was doing within a particular aspect of the business, and then begin to empower them to walk through the process that I took them through while I was alongside of them.

Once I observed the staff walking through that process on several occasions, I would have them come to me with an issue. I would say to them, "Go ahead and solve it and bring me the resolution in the same way I have taken you through it." Afterwards they brought the solution to me and we would talk about it. It got to where I would eventually say to them, "I don't want to know anything about what is going on. If there is an issue, don't bring me a problem. Instead bring me two solutions that you have worked your way through to where the answer can be found." I have taken the time to meet with them once a week for an hour during those three years to observe their solutions to the issues that have arisen. They have now learned the skill of finding two solutions to any problem they face.

After another year of training them on how to process things correctly and bringing all the aspects of finances, staffing, and systems into agreement, I stress that they should only bring me their decisions. I can then trust them and empower them to occupy their part of the business and give them the authority to actually orchestrate within it.

It got to the point where I trusted my senior staff that I gave them the right to discuss different matters with me. As a business person, I do not want to be ruling everything; I want my staff to feel part of something. We would have meetings where we would not even talk about business, we would talk about character things, interpersonal relationships, and what was needed to resolve issues that were more interpersonal within the core leadership of the business. I found that when we did that, it really helped the process for the rest of the staff. When we were trying to put out a fire in a work situation, I brought my staff together and said, "Let us talk about what is going on here." We found that there were issues that were not resolved which created a doorway for the problems to unfold into a mess within our staffing system.

It did not matter what type of problem it was that we were trying to solve. Whenever there was conflict, we knew there was an underlying issue and in turn we would deal with it. And when we were able to identify the gate that allowed something to infiltrate the business, we could get it sorted out. Then the business would actually flow a lot easier.

When I said to my senior staff that I was giving them permission to talk to me personally, this was not an invitation for general friendship. It was an invitation for a relationship connection within a business setting. It did not result in a deep personal relationship in which we would be forever friends and go through life's highs and lows together.

The purpose of this was to build a business culture where there was no animosity amongst the senior level staff and myself. Because when the lower level staff would try to criticise me, my senior staff would defend me. They would say, "No, actually I know him. It does not work like that because I know who he is, and not just because I have worked for him, but because I have worked with him".

I have learned to get my senior staff working with me, not for me. They recognise the authority and the government within the business. And through relational connection and permission in training, it makes it easier for them to function properly as senior staff. They know that if they have things they need to talk to me about, they can speak freely, as they have been empowered by me to do so without fear of losing their job.

One of the ladies on my senior staff approached me after I had been away and asked to see me. This was after I had been in and out of the business for three weeks as I had been traveling and then returned to the business the next day after coming home. She sat me down and said, "I have some things I want to talk to you about. When you come back from being overseas, you are tired and you seem to be a bit snappy with comments like 'I want this done' and 'I want you to do it now'. It is not helpful for the staff and me if you are like that; we know what we need to do. What I would love for you to do is when you come home after traveling, please don't come to work for the two days following, because on the third day you seem to be normal again."

If I had not given my staff empowerment and I had not purposely built a relational connection with them in that capacity – not in a deep friendship way, but as a business task-oriented entity – she would not have had the confidence and or felt safe, knowing that I would not fire her for speaking her mind. I had given her empowerment to run the business aspects and I was not going to fire her just because she spoke up on a matter. So not only was it helpful for her, but it was helpful for me. I would come back home and ring the office and say, "Hi, I am home" and she would say to me, "See you in two days, Ian."

I find that there are times when a husband and wife can get a bit cranky with each other. Things from your personal life can apply to every facet of life, not just business. And like there are times as husband and wife when we seem to get a little snippy with each other, you can also get like that in business, where people are cranky towards one another.

My wife and I have this agreement that if I am like that, she will bring me a glass of water to drink. It is a scientific fact that if the body is dehydrated, the ability to think correctly is not fully functional. If the body does not have enough water (*i.e.*, is dehydrated), it is limited in its ability to carry information properly. If either my wife or I are like that, we can bring the other one a cup of water without having to say anything, and we would recognise what the issue was. We take it like a man. You know, put on the big boy undies and just drink your glass of water. There is no communication needed. Taking and drinking it would be the sign that we agree that we need to settle down without having to say anything. We do not make a big deal out of it.

I told my staff at work about the water and there were times when I would be very snappy and my senior staff member would just get up and bring me a glass of water. They would put it on my desk and just look at the glass of water without words until I drank the glass of water. For me it was a helpful little thing that made my business run more smoothly.

There are some things that you can do if your business is not centred in your core. The first thing I learned is how to use my imagination in pictures of my business to allow it to find a place within my heart and for me to be within my business.

Since I travel quite a lot, the first thing I had to do was to get my wife and family in my heart. I learned this in my home. This is a practical thing that applies to every aspect of life. Foremost, when I am away from my wife, I hold her in my heart. I take the picture of her that is placed in my Bible and daily look at it and hold her face in my mind and hold her in my heart. That way when I am away from her, every person I see that is of the opposite sex, I see through the latticework of my wife's face. This keeps me centred and focused properly.

I learned to do that with my children as well. I hold them in my heart. I love them, want the best for them, yearn after them, and think about them. I always want the best for them, so I engage them. Because they are in my heart, I learned how to do this and actually began to see what they were doing. There were times when I would see them, and I would ring them up and say: "Hi, how did it go today?" And they would say: "Good,

Dad". After a while they realized that when Dad rang, it was because he had seen something that they were doing, and it was naughty. And now Dad was going to tell them off because he "sees". The reason I see is because I want to. I see out of desire and the design that YHVH has given me to be in authority over what He is doing with me, but also to be within it. And since they are within me and I am within them, I can feel them.

Because of what I learned with my family, I also started doing that with my business. When I would go away, I used pictures of my business in my imagination. We can use our imagination, by the way, as long as it is sanctified and not vain. I would hold my business pictures: the plant room, the facilities, the offices, the staff that were there, the register, the till, the gym, and the things that were going on within the business. Eventually I got it in my heart where I could use my imagination, sit over the business and actually look into the different areas. What I began to realise is that YHVH was showing me stuff when I was away that was going on in my business, because it was in my heart. I engaged that place within me, to the point where I was having authority over it. I was able to speak into it, even when I was not present in it. I learned that by first doing it within my family.

By engaging in that process, I could ring one of my senior staff who was involved with all the different rooms and say, "Hi, this is going on with the salt chlorinator" or "This needs to be fixed. If we don't, this is what is going to happen." They would ring me and ask: "How on earth did you know that?" I would say, "Well, you know I am a little bit freaky..." because my staff used to talk about me – this weird guy that sees stuff and does weird stuff. That is all good, as far as I am concerned.

This took about six months of practice to do. It did not just happen because one day I suddenly decided to do it. It took me time to establish the pathway and learn how to access some of this.

It is amazing when we operate and function in this way, and how safe the environment becomes for staff. They will feel safe within your business. When we do this kind of thing it can build loyalty with your staff. My staff realised that I was going to be watching and when something was wrong, I would ring them up and say: "Hi, this needs to be fixed." I used to do this all the time with my staff. I would just ring them and tell them stuff. Sometimes I would love to have been a fly on the wall in my staff room, when they were talking about their boss and the stuff he does.

I have also found that I need to brood over my business, to enfold it within me and learn how to occupy it. It is about governing and overshadowing to supervise with the authority that YHVH has already given me.

If we think about Adam (man and woman) as an example, they were commissioned to govern the earth. As beings in complete union, how can they govern the whole earth? Christ changed it from being a man and a woman to wherever two or three agree. *"Again I say to you that if two of you agree on earth concerning anything that they ask, it will be done for them by My Father in heaven"* (Matthew 18:19 NKJV). But the earth was enfolded within them, giving them the capacity to overshadow the earth. Due to this they could be both up in Eden and down here on the earth simultaneously. They could be above the earth and on the earth. They were above it and on it, governing it from all different facets while sitting over it, overshadowing it. They were looking onto the earth while sitting above it, at the same time looking out over the earth to establish what was needed upon the earth. This is how I learned the process.

One other aspect that I have found to be very helpful is to engage with the angelic realm that sits over your business. It is important to engage with the angelic realm and to involve them in our businesses. I purposely invite the angelic realm to get involved with my business. Here is an example of this.

I took over a company whose facility (I did not own the asset, but I owned the company that rented the facility) had an external fence made up of large panes of heavy-duty glass. We were right next to a rocky shore that had all different sizes of stones on it. Within the first three weeks of me engaging with that business, we had nine or ten panes of tough, thick glass broken by vandals throwing stones and rocks at the glass. These glass panes were expensive.

It took me twenty-one days to realise that I needed to bring some government in. I determined to engage the situation, sitting over it, using my imagination and sitting over my business. I began by sitting over the boundary line, engaging with the boundary line, and putting a restrictive boundary around the outside of my business so that no one would see the glass. I purposed that no one would throw stones at the glass and I released the angelic realm to disrupt anything that would try to cause damage to the glass. I set a boundary and I began to govern it. It is important to establish boundaries when engaging with the angelic realm. They will want to know what you want to happen from a place of maturity. The degree of specificity that you require is the degree they respond with. The more details, the better they can respond. This is not about our calling, it is about us setting boundaries as sons.

From that point on, in the nine years that I had that business, only two panes of glass were broken. Someone did a wheelie in a car in the middle of the car park, ran into one of the posts that held the glass in place and shattered the two pieces of glass on either side of the post. That was not something I ever dreamed would happen. Who would think that someone would do a wheelie and hit a pane of glass by jumping over the edge of the pavement just high enough to run into the post? It was something I did not realise I had to govern. For nine years I governed and established the angelic realm over that business. I established my occupation of that arena, governing it and sitting over the top of it. The day my contract terminated I uplifted all that had been released during my period there and moved my governmental mountain out from that facility, releasing the angelic realm from its function and role under my government. When all the staff left on the last night, my wife and I and my three children all got together. We packed up my mountain; we packed up the angelic realm; we packed up the angelic covering, and took it with us.

I have done teachings on some of this stuff about how to move and pack up your mountain. We packed this thing up, moved it and established it back into my own mountain at home. I unfolded it back within my business mountain, storing it with things that I have plans for in the future. That way in the future when I engage with another business, I can unpack that governing mountain territory canopy over the new business. I do not have to set it up all over again. I can just unpack what I have already established.

After I packed up my mountain that night and moved it out, there were four panes of glass broken at the facility. For the next six weeks, they had glass broken every night around the facility. I find this stuff fascinating in its outworking, revealing the role we have in governing the simple things like the boundary of my business, especially when I see things like that happen.

I have found it helpful to find out what YHVH is wanting to do with our business at its inception. We have to brood over it while engaging the angelic realm. There is a difference between your dreams about your business and what you are thinking about concerning it, and what YHVH is dreaming about for you for your business. These are two totally different realities. I have found it very helpful to sit and engage with the heart of YHVH, just holding the business before Him, setting my heart to observe what His dreams are for it for me. If my mind and my heart are filled with my own things then it becomes very difficult for us to see the things that YHVH wants. It is a conundrum that many of us have to walk through, coming to the place of maturity in how to operate in this. It takes lots of practise as usual.

Now, I am going to talk about one of the businesses we had that failed. I found that engaging in business stuff like this, I always had dreams about what I would love for my business and its outworking in a practical way. I did not realise that I could do what I am now doing in ministry. I thought you had to be a pastor to do ministry stuff like traveling and conference speaking, because that was all I knew. I traded into my religious belief system, that being a pastor was the only way to do ministry. How wrong I was! YHSVH had to take me on a journey to deal with that in my own life.

While I was employed in another's business, I began to think about owning my own business. We wanted to start a fitness centre. We did a massive market research study of fifteen thousand people in the area, and roughly sixty percent of the people said if there was a gym in the area they would join it. That meant that over eight thousand people would be using our gym. As there were no other gyms in the area, I felt very confident after seeing the results of the business study.

We launched a business and spent a lot of money getting it up and running, and for the first three to four weeks, the gym was doing very well, but very slowly attendance started going down and down. I was saying to the Lord, "Where are all the people?" In the middle of this, YHVH had given me a dream. My dream was that I would become self-sufficient and that I would not have to be employed anymore, but through the supply of the business I could be in ministry. Dreaming of my own business and what would come from it got me very excited about the future. This was not necessarily what YHVH was dreaming about. Remember YHVH is more interested in my character and developing it than He is interested in me dreaming about my future. At that time I did not know the difference between my dreams and YHVH's dreams for me. Since then I have learned, but He had to take me on a journey to unpick the tapestry of my own dreams so that His dreams could be woven into them. He will usually break you out of your dreams by leading you through an environment that causes you to let go of what you dream about, to unlock His dreams in you. Coming to the place of maturity with good character is always YHVH's goal. I will talk about my journey through this process now.

What happened was that very slowly the business went down, down, down and I was working eighty hours a week trying to maintain the business and take care of all the stuff related to the business, while also being employed. My wife and I had invested a large amount of finances into the business.

When I first started that business, I said to YHVH that I needed to know if this was of Him, and He gave me a dream. In the dream I saw His hand come down. It had a piece of bread in it and He said, "When my children ask me for bread I will not give them a stone." To me, that was saying YHVH is happy with what I am going to do, and we are going ahead with it, because I now know that it is going to be a success.

When it was not a success, I started wondering, "Why aren't you doing anything, YHVH? You told me this." It is amazing how our own interpretation of what we see can come out of what we believe God wants, when it is not necessarily what God is saying.

What happened with me was that YHVH took me on a journey to deal with my character and to deal with deep internal things in me. It came to the point where my wife and I were five thousand dollars away from bankruptcy, and we sold the business for a massive loss. We were in very dire straits. I can remember walking around a lake with her and crying. We wanted a weekend away but we only had five dollars between the two of us to have a date. So our date ended up being two cups of coffee. We asked, "Lord, what is going on here?" The Lord told me, "The goal, Ian, is not money for you to go into full-time ministry. The goal is to develop your character so you are strong enough inside to be able to handle the pressure. You must understand that I am your provision, and that I bring the provision to you. You cannot get affirmation and fulfillment out of what you are doing. It must come from me."

I started going through the process of dying to my dream of being financially independent, and learning how to become dependent on YHVH's provision. It took us a year and a half to get out of the debt, as we worked our way through it. Through this time YHVH orchestrated some beautiful circumstances around our lives, where we were able to sow abundantly into others. My wife and I determined that we were going to break this thing. Within one year, we had paid all our debts off, we owned our own house free and clear, and we owned a brand-new car.

Now I am not saying that YHVH is going to do that for you. This was our journey through Him dealing with our lives. The key is He has to deal with our character. The development of your character is so important to YHVH. It is the crucible in which He can work on and in us, so that it empowers Him to sit on the earth upon the shadow that looks like Himself.

My encouragement to you is to just allow YHVH to do what He is going to do inside of you. Allow Him to orchestrate circumstances around your life. He will put you under so much pressure that it will cause you to look at your life and where you are, because He does not want any of us to stay the same.

ACTIVATION

Father, thank You that our future looks much better than it does right now. I thank You for the unfolding of everything that You are going to do for us, around us, to us and through us. Father, we are grateful that You are equipping us to be able to do this as business people. We thank You for Your grace in the land of the living, and Your goodness that we are going to be able to move further into what we are doing, in the name of YHSVH. Hallelujah.

CHAPTER 9

THE MYSTERY OF
BUSINESS

Our connection to YHVH as His sons and our walk as business people must be considered. As believers, and as a body of believers worldwide, we have lived separated, compartmentalised lives. We have our work life, our business life, our church life, and then we have our God life. Weaving all these lives together so there is no separation between them is essential. My connection with the presence of YHVH while dwelling in His world has been the vital ingredient that has enabled just such a unity to happen for me.

Many people do not realise that Christ tore the veil for the purpose of giving us unrestricted, unlimited access into His world. We can be participants in this world while carrying out our responsibilities as sons in His world. We too often only focus on the earth, but the earth is just one planet that is part of a solar system and galaxy out of an estimated two trillion galaxies, which make up only thirty-five percent of the known universe. All of it was created by YHVH for our shared responsibility. We need to understand the process of going in through the veil, then being able to go into or ascend to YHVH to experience His presence from that position. It is different than here on Earth where we are limited in time and space.

"After saying these things, Jesus was lifted up into heaven and sat down at the place of honor at the right hand of God!" (Mark 16:19 TPT). YHSVH is seated at the right hand of the Father. So, if I am in Him, I can also be at the right hand of the Father. My perspective in Him observing creation, and my position as a son in Christ seated in heavenly places, enables me to administrate what is necessary, which enables me to influence what is down here. It has taken me twenty years to learn how to do this: it did not just happen in one day. I am a new creature, which means I am the new species on the block. I am going to be a new creature – no longer just human – if you want to frame it like that. *"Therefore if anyone is in Messiah, he is a new creation. The old things have passed away; behold, all things have become new"* (2 Corinthians 5:17 TLV).

I had to learn who I was and what my function was: whether I play a role there or if I just go to Him and worship Him. To me, Heaven would be a very boring place if all I did forever was just worship. There is so much to take care of. I have majored on the issue of responsibility regarding my relational connection with the presence of YHVH. The necessity of my character development is to not be so spiritual, but at the same time be spiritual enough, so that I can do what is necessary here in creation and live it out at a practical level.

YHVH shut down our overseas ministry for almost two years. In that time, I turned my heart to business. I thought I would be a business man for the rest of my life. All ministry had closed down, so I said to Him, "If you are not going to open the doors, Father, then I am just going to plow away with what is in my hands. I am going to work at it this year and take everything that I know and apply it to business." I did that. Over a two-year period we started a couple of businesses and ran them successfully.

One of the key things I have had to learn is how to make decisions and know that YHVH is with me. A key component to that as a process is to not be standing still, just waiting. If I am standing still and waiting to know what my next step is, or just waiting for YHVH to do something, I will not be moving anywhere. I will be like a ship in the sea without its motor running. It just lists from side to side and is blown about by every wind and tidal movement that comes because there is no power to drive the ship forward and to bring direction through the rudder. Direction can only come through positive movement. You can only steer a moving ship. *"Go therefore and... remember! I am with you always..."* (Matthew 28:19–20 TLV). YHSVH did not say for us to go and then He would do it all for us. I have learned that if the Word is true in what it says, and I believe it is, then all I have to do is put one step in front of another knowing that YHVH has called me to be responsible for every aspect of my decisions. Then I start to move in a direction that becomes a part of what is happening around me. I have always had that attitude in my functionality within business life.

I am completely and utterly fascinated with the reality that when YHVH is with us, it does not necessarily mean everything is going to be nice and comfortable. I have had to go through dealing with issues in my life such as the need for affirmation from people, and the need for affirmation to come from what I was providing for my wife. I have had to ask myself, "Why do I love the Lord? Why do I want to do a certain activity? What are the deep-rooted motives of my heart?" When I do not deal with those things, YHVH will take me down a pathway that seems amazing until pressure comes. Then suddenly I have to face the issues in my life so that He can take me on to maturity.

No Longer a Child

One of the things that I love about YHVH is that the Word says, *"God is love"* (1 John 4:8 NKJV). We think that it is all nice and gushy just sitting on His lap, but that is for a child, not for a mature son. A mature son hugs his dad, but also has an opinion – a place of discussion. He is not a little baby sucking his thumb on his dad's lap anymore, but is a functional part of the family. My whole objective is to come to maturity, to become a functional part of the family in Heaven – and to have a part in that family means taking responsibility not just for my spirit-life, but for all that YHVH has given me. This brings us back to the discussion of business.

When I am connected and have a vibrant, living, relational yoke with YHVH as a son, I am able to have face-to-face discussions with Him. There are times when I sit with YHVH across a council table and we discuss subjects I do not understand, but that I need an understanding of. Scripture refers to these as the councils of YHVH: *"...listen in on God's secret council..."* (Job 15:8 EXB). For me to be able to participate in such a council session, there are things that I need to have dealt with first – things like fear inside of me and questioning if YHVH is going to kill me if I say no to Him or if I express my own opinion. Do I even have an opinion? Do I have a voice in all of this? There is also the issue of surrender. (I have no problem with that at all.)

The only way you learn to take responsibility is through vibrant communication with Him. *"In the same way that iron sharpens iron, a person sharpens the character of his friend"* (Proverbs 27:17 VOICE). If I don't allow YHVH to sharpen me in those areas and from that position, then it is all a one-way relationship. Instead, an open-face discussion which involves collaboration, communion, and connection with God is vital.

The only way to do this is through Christ. I do not want somebody to assume that I do not go to YHSVH. The only way you can come to the Father is through Christ. That is the foundation: access comes through the blood of YHSVH. I speak frequently about my connection with YHVH because of the responsibility I have as a father in everything I do. A father's job is to literally replace himself in the community. It is the reason he trains his son to be mature and to take responsibility. Then when the son does something, he will be able to follow it through as though the father is with him wherever he is. YHSVH was no different, so we are no different. YHVH is with us wherever we are. We are just not conscious of that because we have chosen to live outside of that consciousness with God. When I move, I know YHVH is with me because I have a vibrant relationship with Him: that is my function within what I do here in creation. Out of that relationship comes the flow of the realm of the Kingdom. For the Father to follow through and release what is necessary depends on my relational connection. He's not going to release something to someone who is immature, who merely thinks they have something. The question is, have we taken responsibility in YHVH's house?

Fifteen or twenty years ago, I started talking about the courtrooms of heaven and their function. Learning them has been a ten- or twelve-year process. I started teaching it as I was learning about the function of my responsibility within YHVH's house and His kingdom, being seated at the table of seventy, and then being involved in the Sanhedrin of the government of YHVH's world. It did not happen overnight just because one day I decided that I was going to engage with YHVH and He was going to be with me. It was about maturing, and maturity takes time. For a rabbi, it takes something like thirty-five years of walking through all he has to learn before he is recognised within the community as having enough internal life to move as a rabbi. Even then, there are historically only three rabbis at a time in Israel, and he cannot become a rabbi until one of them passes or releases his role. I see this as the same for us coming into maturity as the sons of YHVH. He can release His functions to us, so we can do His job and be a complete reflection of Him, only after our union with Him.

What is Trading?

There is no greater trade than a person giving his life for a friend. *"Greater love hath no man than this, that a man lay down his life for his friends"* (John 15:13 KJV). Christ laid the pattern as the ultimate in giving so that we could have everything. In giving everything, He was promoted to a position so great within creation and YHVH's will to be seated by His Father in a major position of government. That sets an example for me for the way I should be. There are many interesting aspects of trading: trading is not limited to financial application. Trading is one of the most contentious issues that has developed out of anything we do. People would rather just give something at the end of a meeting in an offering than to actively engage during a session.

Trading is about an exchange process. I recognized early on in my life that the law of sowing and reaping is involved in trading as it arcs together with honour and favour. Without the law of sowing and reaping, you will not find favour. My wife and I determined to be generous, but hidden. In that place of hiddenness, we gave in a manner that would be fully for YHVH's sole audience and not for the eye-service of people. We chose that kind of lifestyle, and many years later realised we were actually trading within honour in a different way. We were not just giving, we were doing it purposefully to leverage favour with YHVH, which is what trading really is when done in the right attitude and heart.

The favour of YHVH sitting on your life is like gold refined in a fire. You experience it when you have walked through your life's trials. Being able to engage with the treasuries of Heaven is evidence of Zion – it is the favour of YHVH being seen and revealed in the treasuries on the earth. This has to do with riches and all the things associated with the wealth transference that so many people have been talking about for the last twenty years. We have not seen a lot of it happen because there has been neither favour nor honouring in the right way as far as I am concerned. The new catchword honour has so often been used as another word to replace control.

Trading became a reciprocal thing for me. I realised that both my wife and I had a continual laughter about it. We would ask ourselves if we were going to give a certain amount. Three weeks later, we would get a cheque for four times that amount. When we chose to give our money away, it came back to us in greater measure. One month, we decided to give a rather large amount of money away to someone. After that, the pattern of my website sales just for that month went up one hundred percent compared to what they normally were, which was about two hundred percent of what we gave away. We saw this pattern repeat over and over. We have learned through experience that to leverage YHVH's trading floor, we need to do so out of the abundance of YHVH. Leveraging must come out of not just generosity, but of union, connection, and lack of desire to perform or be seen by others. In the secret place for the audience of One, we find relational connection. From that place, the approval of YHVH will be seen in the physical world and made open for others to see.

I have learned YHVH is never in a hurry. There is usually something He wants to deal with in our lives or there may be a timing issue. Scripture shows us that He is going to build of us a great nation. *"My heart's desire is to make you into a great nation..."* (Genesis 12:2a TLV). It may start with one person per generation, but it will increase. He is not in a hurry and He will do what He has to do to bring it into being.

When we allow the environment to rule over us, we choose to live in stress. A key component of governing is finding a place of rest. I have learned to handle stress through engaging with YHVH in the middle of situations. Then the pressures do not affect me, even though they may be raging on the outside.

In a teaching called "Presence-Driven Warfare," I refer to the way David talked about how YHVH prepares a table for us.[14] *"You prepare a table before me in the presence of my enemies"* (Psalm 23:5 NKJV). We think enemies refers to people who assail us, but our enemy is anything that takes us out of the peace of God. I have learned what it is to sit at that table in the midst of turmoil around me.

One of the greatest treasures I found was when YHVH took me through a circumstance where a company I had invested in went into liquidation and I lost an exceedingly large amount of money. During that experience, I went through the mental gymnastics of trying to find a solution and trying to see how to find my way past what was going on right in front of me. I went into court and allowed myself to be judged, which exposed areas of vulnerability. I found that if I allowed the circumstances around me to rally me, I would start to go down a spiral vortex, which had to do with the way I mentally would look at something and try to find a resolution. To look at something to see where it is going to go can become a fantasy. Using your imagination to try and find a resolution to something that is a fantasy leaves you with fantasies working together with no reality. I found myself in this spiral for three months. I was going down further into depression while trying to figure out what the noise was, asking myself how I was going to solve a problem that I knew I could not solve. The surrendering part was realising I had no solution. The only place I could find a solution was to first of all find a place of peace with YHVH.

I started shutting my brain down from all the thoughts that were assailing me, telling me it was my own choice to try and find resolutions to the problem. I started to consciously turn toward the presence of YHVH and His faces. I began to walk toward them and suddenly, through the involvement with the court system of the government of Heaven allowing YHVH to judge my thoughts and the intent of my heart, I found there

---

[14] Available on sonofthunder.org

was no intention of evil in me. I took responsibility for the evil that came, even though it was not my fault. I began to walk my way through all these things that were not my issues or responsibility. I was prepared to take responsibility for them. I openly told the Lord I needed His help in the middle of this.

At the end of that time, my wife and I made a choice. Even though we had contracts with people who had invested with us, we decided to pay back the principle that they had given us to invest. We did not have to do it. But it was, for me, one of the highest forms of trading that enabled kingship treasure to materialise. It was a trade of honour: there was no requirement to do it, except for honour and because of YHVH Himself.

You make a choice to find favour through honour. We made a conscious choice to begin to do that. It has taken us three years to pay back to the people who invested with us. We did not have to do it. It has been a journey that my wife and I have gone through to begin to see the favour of YHVH come out of honour, but then because of the favour, honour is coming. Because we have died, we now find new life. We have walked our way through turmoil that pressed in on us. You can choose to stay here and engage with the pressure, but you do not have to. You can go into God and come through the veil. You can position yourself to see into the presence of YHVH who is sitting over the top of it, and you can make it look up to you, instead of you continuing on its level. It is a huge relief to be brought out of that kind of situation.

The Men and Women in White Linen

I have done hours of teaching on the men in white linen.[15] Teaching these kinds of things gives a foundation to be able to engage. Everything is about relationship: I choose relationship above knowledge. By finding relationship, I get to speak with the person and gain knowledge because I talked with them. I

---

[15] Available on sonofthunder.org

did not just read some information. I find what is written in the Word can be sketchy compared to the full measure of what was observed or actually going on. What has been written is a record to help us uncover more, but we tend to see it as complete in itself. In doing this, we can miss out on so much more that is involved and related to it.

I see the Word as a gateway of entry into connectivity. This is how I purposefully set my heart to engage with the men and women in white linen, the cloud of witnesses, the ancient ones, the ever-living ones, the desert fathers, and with some of the other beings that are in YHVH's world – because they are the same as we are going to be and are. The intent of the heart is a key ingredient yoked with the desire to turn and build relationships. Whenever I have a spiritual experience, I do not have it as just a "Wow!" experience and try to figure out what it was all about or try to get an interpretation for it. I try to engage and see what is going on. For me, the encounter is an unlocking of a doorway to something, not the final resolution. I have found by itself it is wholly incomplete. I have learned to go in and not to try to understand, but to honour the mystery of that which I did not observe when it occurred. I take what is revealed, and out of that place of honour, find a way to engage with and connect to it in the right way. The Word says to *"Taste and see that the Lord is good..."* (Psalm 34:8a NLT).

Some of the men and women in white linen are people whom I have become very interested in while I read the Bible. I will go into the wine room in YHVH's mountain, where the racks of wine are stored, which hold the record of the glory of YHVH poured out in their lives. The record is held in heaven in the form of wine, which is a treasure. I go into the wine room, find a wine and a record, then drink their wine so I can taste and then begin to see. I find that process so helpful to entangle myself with them. I am not talking to the dead (necromancy as some would call it), I am talking to the living. I am not talking to them in this world here, but in YHVH's world.

Please do not get me wrong. My functionality in all of this is not to be seated on the earth inside my lounge and have someone from Heaven stand in front of me and talk to them. I am in YHVH's world, in His Kingdom and realm. I am in His house, in the chambers of His Kingdom and of His house in His mountain, engaging relationship there. Out of their understanding, I engage with them in that arena and I set my heart to know them. The way you start is to begin to honour someone's life. You begin to honour who they were, what they did, their function and the revelation of what YHVH gave them.

I entangle myself with them and the Word that describes their function and what they were doing. I begin to entangle myself around them to unlock my heart, which is always to build relationship. It often can take months at a time to build a relational connection for even what I would call an encounter. I am already in an encounter because I am in His Kingdom. I am in the courts and governmental chambers, and in whatever way I need to be within YHVH's world. I seek for a depth that is not in my current experience because I want relationship. So often, I would very slowly find that an awareness would come of those people I had set my heart to engage with. Then one day, there is a presentation when suddenly I recognise them in a crowd. I go up to talk to them all day, or they come up to me and introduce themselves. Sometimes it is hilarious! They watch everything you do because you set your heart to engage. This is the same with the issue of honour, which has always been there as a prime factor. Honour opens a door that pursuit does not.

YHVH Giving and Stewardship

In the Old Testament, you owed the tithe which meant you gave YHVH ten percent of your money with no variable choice. In the New Testament, YHVH owns the money, and you ask Him how much do you keep. I realised that through the order of Melchizedek. Through my identity and function related to YHVH within creation, I am not just the keeper or presenter of something. I am actually a complete steward of everything that YHVH has given me to steward correctly. Understanding stewardship becomes a vital ingredient to our functionality in our position as sons and as business people. It is not so much a question of how much we give, but rather how much do we keep. We choose to ask YHVH how much we need to live off of and what to do with the rest of it.

Being a steward comes back to the arena of responsibility. The Word is very clear and there are many parables YHSVH taught about being responsible for what is in our hands. Even though we may have a small amount, YHVH can give us more. If we are not good stewards of what we have, He will not be able to give us more. Stewarding has become a vital ingredient to everything going on and it has unlocked doors so that we can function properly. Being a steward does not just mean stewarding our finances, it means stewarding our time, what we do, and how we spend our day in our relationship with YHVH. We are to be stewards of our interpersonal relationships with those YHVH has put close to us. While being a steward of the body of Christ and of revelation, we are to be a steward of our body. Being a steward involves every area. The more we are stewards of what YHVH has given us, and the better stewards we are, the more YHVH can unlock for us until we do not just become the steward, we become the owner.

We need to be stewards to others and all that YHVH has given us responsibility for. YHVH has shown me not to live a separate life from those who are my partners. We are co-heirs with Christ, which means we are both participants in everything I do. I have a conscious awareness that YHVH is sitting with YHSVH and the Holy Spirit here with me in everything I am doing. That awareness works all the way down into my deep personal life, including walking in His way with my relationships with other people. I am aware that YHVH is here with me, but that is because I have consciously turned into Him and engaged with Him for so many years that I do not need to consciously engage anymore. I am subconsciously aware of that engagement on a continual basis because I have built the pathway for that connectivity. By having Him as a partner, I can turn to Him and discuss the things that need resolution. If I want to know business and financial answers, I talk with Melchizedek. Do not talk with Noah or Daniel about finances, but talk to them about other matters that they were schooled in. If you want to know how to handle extreme wealth, go talk to Solomon. A lot of people think that he lost his way. He did, but in the end, Solomon repented when he said that all this was vanity. *"The words of the Preacher, the son of David, king in Jerusalem. 'Vanity of vanities,' says the Preacher; 'Vanity of vanities, all is vanity'"* (Ecclesiastes 1:1–2 NKJV).

It is amazing to see what Solomon did as he stewarded the wealth of YHVH in the land of the living. At this point in time, we are having to labour with our hands to get things done and to do things. I often wonder and imagine what it is going to be like in the future when we need something. Perhaps all we will have to do is breathe it into existence, materialising matter out of desire and intent, because we learned how to be a steward of what YHVH has released to us. Imagine not having to go through the process of figuring out how to build something anymore. Instead, imagine being able to see your project in your heart, know what it looks like, and then construct and build it. YHVH has given us creative abilities. The more we steward what we have here and understand it, the more it will be able to be unlocked. This includes the knowledge of YHVH within it, and His voice that frames it, right down to the molecular, atomic and subatomic levels and structure until it is able to be physically manifested.

Solomon made gold and silver so abundant that the streets were paved with it. We think that maybe he mined it, but I believe he made it as the Word says. Go and talk to them, find out how they did it: we do not have to go down the road that they went down to get the finished product. They already opened the pathway for us. That is why the Word is so powerful. It has already opened up the way for us. Through relationship, we have a shortcut available right now but we still must walk through the process.

I think some of the church system has forgotten that YHSVH tore the veil and that He tore it for a reason. This has given us unrestricted access into His presence here in the Kingdom of the earth. Many caught in an older age or through religious exercise would rather stand outside the veil, beat their drum, make a lot of noise, and ask YHVH to come down rather than go through to the other side themselves and build relationship with Him in His world. Sometimes we are afraid because of a fear of rejection or shame, or a fear of being unworthy. These are very normal responses for a person before they have gone through the veil. Once we experience the grace, goodness and the love of YHVH from the other side of the veil, all that changes. The greatest thing about the grace of God is that He has given us unrestricted, unhindered access. The key with this is that it is not our job to make ourselves clean. This is what Christ does when we go and present ourselves to Him. YHSVH is our High Priest: He makes us clean through what He has done through the cross for us. That is the foundation I come from. I go into YHVH's realm through the veil.

We as a species have no idea of the value YHVH has placed on us here in creation. I do not think we have come to the point where we recognise ourselves as the only ones that have ever been created who can actually host the very person and presence of YHVH. We can take on His image and bear His likeness and image, as scripture says: *"as we have borne the image of the earthly..., so shall we also bear the image of the heavenly..."* (1 Corinthians 15:49 NIV). There is an intrinsically woven fabric within humanity within our DNA to be able to bear the record of God within us.

When we engage and remain in the presence of YHVH in His world, there is nothing so fulfilling than to find His joy. The

Word says that YHVH sits in heaven and laughs. *"He who sits in heaven laughs!"* (Psalm 2:4 TLV). We have almost missed the reality that YHVH is happy. We have a vague image of Him sitting on the throne, which is really only one aspect of His function within Heaven. So often, YHVH laughs at me about things that I feel are serious. He laughs at me because He sees me doing mental gymnastics to figure out what He is saying. This relational union makes everything down here worth it. It is worth the price, because the inheritance we have is worth labouring for and being a steward over.

Everything comes back to stewardship. What is within our hearts is the measure of provision that YHVH is going to bring to us. It does not come out of you doing things to position yourself on earth. It comes out of your relational connection and positional function within Heaven. Riches and the over-flowing abundance will come to the seat of a king in Heaven. If we are not on that seat, we will never be able to display it. This seat in Heaven will be the only avenue that will be used to fully materialise wealth flowing unrestricted onto the earth. There are ways to unlock it down here, including refining your char-acter, your connection to the Spirit of Wisdom, through rela-tionship with Melchizedek and finally an active engagement with function in trading.

So, go: do amazing business things, find the place of rest, learn how to operate and function in this world by breathing Heaven into the earth.

CHAPTER 10

THE SPIRITUAL PERSPECTIVE OF BUSINESS

I am aware that there are those who debate whether a business can be spiritual or not. Some say it is not possible. But due to our relational connection with YHVH, everything we do has a spiritual component. The realm of Kingdom government we operate in, particularly as an employer or business owner, provides the spiritual dimension.

One of the first hallmarks to position us to become kings within the marketplace is our internal character development. Being a king or priest is first dependent on the relational connection we have with YHVH. That relationship produces the ability to manifest the Kingdom down here in the marketplace.

Taking part in business and being involved in marketplace connections comes down to the heart of a person.

We need to walk through the process of being positioned in a place of rest. From there, we can engage in Kingdom business. In reading about King Solomon in the Bible, I noticed that nothing seemed to disturb him. Everything he functioned out of was from a Kingdom realm of peace. From that place, and through his connectivity with the presence of YHVH, he was able to manifest what YHVH wanted here in creation. In any environment that creates disruption, we need to find and be at peace in our conduct and connectivity, as well as in our internal character. Many have not developed the necessary character to handle what they have now in business.

I believe that in the age to come in Zion, we will be able to operate like Solomon. When he ascended, he made gold and the cedars of Lebanon abundant. I believe the ability to manifest gold – and whatever we may need – is coming for us in the future. The connectivity of the way we operate now in the priesthood in which we are administering will open up the gate for YHVH to intervene in the circumstances within our businesses. It is our position as priests that makes business a spiritual thing.

Even though business is part of the physical realm, it is also part of the spiritual realm. It is the voice of YHVH framing creation here through us measuring photons of light to form solid objects. It all comes out of the Kingdom spirit realm. Depending on where our reality sits, anything physical is a spiritual thing. We can position ourselves to be able to look into what we are doing here and see what our focus needs to be. Moving and functioning out of our position in Heaven, not moving to and fro in our position on earth, allows us to be able to observe Heaven's perspective of our businesses. It gives us insight into what needs to be changed and what areas need to be influenced, spoken over, or gathered in.

Everything around us is spiritual, but it also has a practical application. A person living from the physical perspective will fight to keep their position. They do not want to acknowledge that there is something or someone above themselves, especially if they hold onto things in their heart or have areas in their life they have not dealt with. If we are pleasing people, we will find that YHVH will put pressure on us to deal with things that do not belong in our life. This is one reason why I tell people to deal with anything in their life that does not please the Father, because YHVH wants vessels He can use that are not corrupt.

There is no doubt that we are on the forefront of wealth transference now. In the past I heard so much about it that I did not want to hear any more. There is a time when the world will come to the light of our shining: kings will come, bring their riches and lay them at our feet. A day is coming when all of this will be fully physically manifested here in creation, but I do not believe it is for us just yet.

What I do know is that finances will not come to a person, they will come to a position in the Kingdom of Heaven. That is why understanding the order of Melchizedek is so important for the body of Christ. It is about becoming kings and priests. As kings we must sit on our thrones, learn how to govern, and practice demonstrating authority over our environment and circumstances. We have to be able to legislate, decree, speak and operate as kings.

YHVH is looking to see if we will take responsibility in His world. Authority will not come to your position on earth until it is revealed through you first in Heaven. Connectivity in Heaven is the vital ingredient. It is the relational, functional capacity we have as fully immersed sons of YHVH who are able to engage in His Kingdom world, and from that we are able to administer it down here on earth. Our perspective must always be from Heaven into earth. It must not be about moving laterally down here. If we move laterally, we will always run into problems. We need to be engaged in the living, Kingdom world of

YHVH's governmental seat to be able to look from Heaven into creation for what needs to happen here on earth.

There is a transition coming for us to enter through Zion's gate, where we will take our seats and begin to govern creation. The seat that Ezekiel sat on (Ezekiel 1) and the function of that seat was for an immature son. While Ezekiel 1 relates to the earth, the other side in Ezekiel 10 directly relates to the governmental dimensions of the Kingdom realm associated with YHVH's world. Whatever goes on in that Kingdom world has a major influence over the earth, and it will eventually affect us here in a coming display of change.

Favour and honour will be incredibly important in our walk. It is not just about having favour to get things: honour helps release that favour. Several years ago, there was a lot of talk about the culture of honour. While all of that was amazing, a lot of focus was placed on honouring uphill, so to speak, with no emphasis on honour being returned downhill. It was all about honouring those in leadership. But honour should also flow downhill to the least of those amongst us. We need to honour the least in such a way that they can become the leader. Then we do not have to be the leader anymore because of who they are in their identity in YHVH. Allowing the least to be more than you are is an important operation within the Kingdom. The Lord's thinking is upside-down to the world. We need to embrace the thinking in the heart of YHVH as this Kingdom realm begins to unlock for us. Solomon's display of the way his servants were dressed and all those that were connected to his tables shows that the least can be full of honour and joy.[16]

We need to address heart issues concerning the source from which we receive our sense of affirmation. We need to be sure our affirmation does not come from what we are doing, or from people seeing us do spiritual things. It needs to come from our

---

[16] 1 Kings 10:5 tells us that the Queen of Sheba was amazed by Solomon's servants' clothes. The traditional belief is that she could not tell King Solomon apart from his servants because he dressed them all with the same honour he gave to himself.

sense of our own personal connectivity with YHVH in relationship. Our fulfillment comes from the perspective of doing it for
the audience of One, seeking His approval and not man's. We
should not be concerned about what other people think of us or
what they say about us. People have a lot of opinions. I have
had to learn how to engage with YHVH to the point where others' opinions do not affect me. The Bible says to love your enemy. This is a place of systemic change within the Christian environment that is gradually moving through the body of Christ.

> *"You have heard that it was said, 'You shall love your neighbor
> and hate your enemy.' But I say to you, love your enemies, bless
> those who curse you, do good to those who hate you, and pray
> for those who spitefully use you and persecute you, that you
> may be sons of your Father in heaven..."* (Matthew 5:44 NKJV)

Recently, the Lord has spoken to me very clearly about the
life of His living Word and how every single human functions
as a spirit being. The Bible says, *"The spirit of man is the can-
dle of the Lord"* (Proverbs 20:27 KJV). Even though it may not
be ignited with the presence of YHVH yet, the spirit is still His
life in every single human being. We could not exist as an entity
without our spirit being. It gives us the ability to have life.
When I see someone I dislike, I am learning to reach into and
observe the spark of life that sits in them and to love that piece
in them. I may not necessarily love all of them, but I love that
piece that is in them. I am finding that it is helping me deal
with not liking people. I am a work in progress. The Father
seems only too happy to put people in front of me for me to
learn to like, to build my internal character.

When insecurity is in our life, we may act out of that insecurity. When we are insecure, our fulfillment comes out of someone else's affirmation of us, not from the affirmation within our
relationship with YHVH. On a positive note, in some ministries' leadership I have found people who surround themselves with others who are truthful. They can openly talk about
the issues in their lives and have iron sharpening iron conver-

sations to get down to the basics without the issue of rejection. *"As iron sharpens iron, so people can improve each other [sharpen their friends]"* (Proverbs 27:17 EXB).

It comes back to love. One of the character traits YHVH is going to unlock for us is love. It is a love that overcomes all, covering a multitude of sin – love for your neighbor and YHVH, love for yourself and love for all the world. YHVH is developing this type of love within the body of Christ so He will be able to do everything He is about to do. I do not think everyone is going to be able to be positioned in that place, but I do believe it is available to everyone. Not everyone wants to die, deal with their issues or build relationships and walk in the Kingdom realm.

Many men and women get caught in the birthing chamber to something more. Sometimes, they get stuck in deliverance or healing, which are fantastic things, but those are examples of the birthing chambers I am speaking about. I have purposed to never get stuck, because there is always going to be more. We need to find our seats in Zion and in our cities. There are amazing things coming that we do not even have words for. We must come into the understanding of the eternal Kingdom realm, which is just the beginning. We do not yet fully understand what will happen from there. A lot of us are still stuck in the Age of the Church and in the Age of the Kingdom, trying to figure out what YHVH is doing down here on the earth instead of what He is doing in Heaven.

YHVH is capable of doing whatever we need to have done, but He has us in position to make this exchange. He has given everything in the ages we have entered: all of Heaven, the ancient ones, the Seven Spirits of the Lord, the Cloud of Witnesses, and also the Men and Women in White Linen. All this has been made available to us to be able to refine our character and tutor us in some of what we do not understand.

When it comes to character, certain things seem obvious. Some people live in snares because they have a negative mindset, while expecting something else. There is a leverage point here. I do not know how to describe it by time, because time does not look the same to me now. The dimensions have something to do with it. I find there are two sides. There are people who have worked hard and have gathered themselves a nest egg. They have gathered some finances, yet they are a little afraid. They want to see things change, but they are afraid to fully engage. They try, but they follow some of Babylon's rules governing the function of bondage in our lives. So it does not seem to work out. On the other side, there are those who are totally vulnerable. They will give everything and will not think anything of it. The two sides are not working well, and they do not necessarily get anything moving, like positive/negative poles on a magnet being forced together.

I believe we are in a season of a necessary leverage point, and I believe YHVH is determined that we do it the right way. We need to overcome the fear of those who have an overflow of abundance or position, and we need to deal with our rejection with wisdom. Then there are those who are vulnerable: they will just do anything, even walk into traps and be robbed. Neither one is effective. I love people who are open and vulnerable, but many of them will lose all their money because they are not very wise. Then there are those who hold onto their money. They have not learned to surrender, which is not very effective either. There is a needed aspect of wisdom in the middle of all of this. Wisdom goes deeper than just having knowledge. It is having a living connection and a vibrant relationship with YHVH, in which you are vulnerable to Him and You allow Him to direct you. Becoming vulnerable to YHVH in these areas helps us unlock and become vulnerable to those around us to be able to build relationships in the right way.

The Kingdom age with its protocols of gifts and giving and sowing and reaping matures us towards becoming stewards of what is in our hands. However, in the Melchizedek Age, it goes beyond being stewards to becoming sons who realise that nothing belongs to us and we are coheirs with Christ, learning how to govern YHVH's world (Romans 8:17). Nothing we have within the Age of Melchizedek belongs to us. It is the place of learning that is going to empower us to be revealed as coheirs – as kings under authority.

Part of being stewards within the Melchizedek Order's function is learning how to become keepers of the wealth and the treasure YHVH releases to us. Relational union with YHVH will give us the ability that will empower us to unlock and retract from circumstances that are destructive and unnecessary. He will help us retract from these circumstances in an appropriate manner, and by doing this, will help us open up things that are good. We will find our connectivity within whatever YHVH is breathing on.

Personally, what I try to do when somebody has financial trouble is to find a point of connectivity within what is happening, so they can buy into that connectivity to help them see YHVH in the middle of their circumstances. That buy-in process is vital to unlocking the treasure of the heart of a person. A person who is too free and easy with their finances loses everything. They need wisdom not to buy into everything that tickles their ear. So often when people buy into things, it is because they hope that what they buy into will cause them to be better off. They look to the security of what they could come into, instead of looking at their source who is YHVH. A choice to surrender to Him as our supply is vital. Surrendering to YHVH is the key.

I can recognise patterns like this in my own early life. I can acknowledge stupid decisions I made through the process, but I would not swap the burning and the character development that came out of it for anything. I am glad I walked through the fire because it helped me deal with my junk. It is very hard to pry the hands and fingers of a controlling person off their finances. Like Ebenezer Scrooge, we will try to hold onto every cent of a dollar and become micro-managers because we are afraid. That fear does not produce much in our character or in our life. It positions us in control of others because of our own fear of losing everything. This is a cycle people get into. This type of person holds onto everything they have instead of being vulnerable to the presence of YHVH. The body of Christ has primarily lived in a poverty framework for so long that a lot of people are left in the position of having no idea who YHVH is anyway.

I think that the leverage point regarding our position is going to come through the visible revealing of the glory of YHVH in our life. People will be drawn to the light of your shining.

> "Adonai will arise upon you,
> and His glory will appear over you.
> Nations will come to your light,
> kings to the brilliance of your rising." (Isaiah 60:2–3 TLV)

It is this shining of light that is going to be the key of every aspect of technology that YHVH is releasing in creation at this point, to help us leverage our future. It is that shining, along with the physical revealing, that will draw men to come to this light. The light will shine, and the finances will be there because kings will be drawn to the light and will lay their riches at your feet.

> "...In My favor I will show you mercy.
> Your gates will be open continually.
> They will not be shut day or night,
> so that men may bring to you the wealth of the nations,
> with their kings led in procession." (Isaiah 60:10–11 TLV)

Our seat from within YHVH's realm will unlock what is necessary for the light to shine through technology and bring financial input. We are going to be able to sit with kings and walk with them as kings ourselves. A king must have financial backing. He has to have finances to do what is needed. David and Solomon are classic examples of this financial overflow. Being a king is not just a spiritual dynamic, it is a practical dynamic as well, revealing the supply of YHVH into all that is needful.

With every business you start, there are always character issues that have to be worked out in connectivity with other people, especially with people you work with. Little details make up the environment to mature you to be able to handle more. To me the issue is faithfulness. The Word says that when you are faithful with little, YHVH will give you much. *"Whoever can be trusted [is faithful] with a little can also be trusted [is also faithful] with a lot, and whoever is dishonest [unjust] with a little is dishonest [unjust] with a lot"* (Luke 16:10 EXB). I think that being faithful with what YHVH has given us, and our handling of people, creates a capacity for YHVH to reveal the "much". Pressure points create that crucible point. The pressure point in the birthing chamber helps to bring character flaws to the surface. Part of the process is moving through the birthing chamber. Being able to move through it requires pressure in the same way a child being birthed does. I do not like the word pushing because it implies something is closed. The key to this is not so much pushing through as it is yielding to YHVH so that the birthing chamber can widen to release what is necessary. These things go deep into the heart of people and touch deep strengths in people's lives.

We are to steward from YHVH's perspective. There have been times we wanted to move things along quickly, and suddenly YHVH would stop whatever was going on. There were other times when we started and failed in some major areas of our life. When I look back at what happened, I would not trade those times for anything. Now I can see the hand of YHVH in them. As a consequence, the latter glory of the house is far greater than it would have been. Even though I am looking at the latter glory of the house that I now have, what I had then was still amazing. There were promises that had been fulfilled and it seemed everything was going well for me. At the time, I did not understand why He stopped it and allowed us to go to the point of bankruptcy. Looking back on it, I understand it was to work character in our lives, to remould deep-rooted issues in my own life about my supply connection with YHVH and my affirmation of what I was not achieving with my hands.

Twenty to thirty years ago, my wife and I started a business with so much promise and background work. We invested large amounts of money into the business. In the first three months, the business did very well. Then it started going downhill. I began working more and more hours, trying to keep the business afloat and keep myself in a position to take care of my young family. I worked twelve hours a day trying to get it all done, until I realised that it was not working. My wife and I had to sit down and look at each other across the table and realise that we might be losing everything. Nothing seemed to be working. We questioned YHVH, wondering what was going on. We reminded Him of all He had promised us at the very beginning. One of the things YHVH showed me was Him putting His hand out in front of me with a gold bar in it and telling me that He would not give His children a stone when they asked Him for bread from Heaven. As it says in scripture, *"For what man among you, when his son asks him for bread, will give him a stone?"* (Matthew 7:9 TLV).

I asked all the whys. I reminded YHVH of my desire for increase so that I could go into ministry. Years later I am glad that I did not get into ministry at that point because YHVH had to deal with stuff inside of my life. What did the experience do to my wife and me? It drew us closer as a couple in a place of brokenness where there was no escape from the pressure. It turned us to YHVH. Slowly, very slowly, we worked ourselves through that process. Then YHVH opened the birthing chamber. Within a year, the debt we had was all paid back. It was like we had to go through that horrible hopelessness, at times only having five dollars a week to spare.

Going through that chamber built character in us. In hindsight, I am glad YHVH took us through it, even though it

brought questions. In the middle of all of it, in the places of encounter for me, I would sit at a table with Him, bawling, trying
to figure out what I did, and questioning why He was doing
this. He would just look at me as if He was completely ignoring
me. He seemed to ignore my condition and what I was going
through. He would look at me like I was normal, and I would
ask if He could see that I was upset. I complained that this was
not nice. But He would look at me carrying on and He would
talk about something else. I imagine I felt like Noah did: after
all, it was almost like He forgot Noah in the boat for one hundred and fifty days. It felt like He forgot me, but He was dealing
with stuff in our lives.

Timing plays an important role. The tumblers are turning
for timing to reposition us by dealing with our character. This
happened with my wife and me, with the end result being a
changed life. Time helps to reposition a whole lot of things in
our lives, especially concerning the opening of the gates of Zion
and its supply to creation. Again, the key is character development.

When all of this begins to unlock in the right way, YHVH
will bring teams of people around us that can begin to administrate some of the overflow within creation. It is not going to be
the normal way of administrating what is going to take place.
When I look at the structure of the Kingdom, it extends from
His throne and mountain, then moves out from there like a
spoke in a wheel. This creates a connectivity to the mountain of
YHVH being blueprinted to the outworking of the spokes to the
rim of the wheel. There will be spokes and wheels and spokes
within wheels. There will come an outworking of relational
business connections which keep coming back to the same
mountain. Because of the supply that comes from the mountain
of YHVH revealed through us in creation, there will always be a
leverage point that comes back to Him.

All we have to do is govern from the mountain and from
within some of those systems through a spoke connected to it,

so that it will develop its own wheel and its own hub system. If you take one piece here to open up another piece there, and open another piece here, then you grow a tree. It is the same way that you grow thoughts inside your brain – it looks similar to the branching of neural connections. It is all interconnected, but it will come back to a mountain because of the Kingdom purpose.

I believe that there will come a structured way to be able to administrate some of the things that YHVH is going to do within creation for us. It is going to be shocking to those who currently have all that is necessary but have not done all that is needful. It is not just about the physical experience of having finances, although it is important and a vital functioning part of the process. In reality, this is about the full development of the human race as a species, to a point that we can do what is needful with our planet and our interplanetary system.

The development of people around us and our connectivity to those people is going to be the key. I dislike the seven mountains teaching because it has taught people to go into completely corrupt mountains. Most of those who have gone into the corrupt governmental mountain have been eaten up and spat out by the system. I believe there is a time when we will be able to build our own mountain regarding the function of the laws of abundance.

Creating an internal, circular pattern with finances is an important process in establishing a successful economy. You build an economy to make it circular so that finances never really leave the house. In the early church people built circular networks in which they only traded with those they were in relational connection with. By doing this an internal, circular financial market started to form. Basically it works like this: I pay you, you pay my guy I am getting things from, he gives me stuff over here, I pay you because I need your service and then you pay him. The money goes around and around, never actually leaving point A. It stays in a closed financial system.

I believe YHVH will empower us to build internal, closed financial systems in which we will trade and engage with one another without having to go to an external, corrupt mountain. That mountain does not need to have influence over what we are doing. Building the system with internal structures is going to be a process. I know of groups of people that have internal, closed financial systems. They all have businesses and all own houses. Their houses are purchased by their main body and then all the people who are in those houses purchase them, which puts them in debt to the main body instead of a corrupt financial system. The money stays within the main body to buy more houses for other people that are involved and working. So, this internal system keeps growing. The more people that enter it, the bigger the closed financial system becomes. I have looked in the past at how to develop some of this but put it aside because it was not time yet. But it is coming.

When I first started to approach the arena of exchange finances and was learning how to get out of the legal system that sits around us, the Lord took us to an old rabbinical man from Israel. He talked about how in ancient Israel you gave alms. People would ask for alms, because they wanted you to give them their portion. This was their right: the law said you had to give alms to the poor. But alms could be given to anyone. So, they started giving each other rabbinical alms so they would not lose anything. The man explained alms were part of the corrupt trading table inside the temple. That is why YHSVH became angry with them, because they were exchanging alms with one another. The temple became a corrupt trading place. I think turning over the money changing tables is going to happen again soon. YHVH is going to flip those tables over again for us. Then, we can engage in what we are supposed to instead of being stuck in the world's system of finances.

I am completely aware that YHVH is trying to move to establish a financial system. The current financial system has taken us to where we are now, to finally reveal itself as a corrupt system that YHVH wants to turn upside down again. It is fascinating to see the emergence of cryptocurrencies as a closed-circuit financial system. I believe that instead of shares or using a currency, major businesses will have the capacity to trade with one another in a closed loop in the future, as a way of exporting and purchasing supplies.

I understand the issues for taxation. I understand the need for countries to have finances to run their economies, but all of this is going to change. Imagine if you could go to the government and ask them what their national debt is, and be able to then manifest the gold to pay it off out of Heaven. When we do this kind of thing, it will give us the ability to have influence and begin to deal with core issues within corrupt systems. I do not know how governments are going to handle it when we can make wealth out of the realm of Heaven. In the meantime, we have to deal with what is around us. I think one of the ways we will deal with what is around us is through the opening of Melchizedek's treasure chamber.

YHVH is trying to work out His plan in the heart of man. Although He will not cross the will of man, He provides the opportunity for our will to be bent toward His will by presenting us with the continued ability to make the right choices. We must realise that we are no longer owners of what we have, but we are keepers and stewards of the measure that YHVH has given us. We do not own it. One of the key transitions that I believe is going to come through the expression of the Melchizedek order, is embracing this realisation. If we are caught in an old system of being a servant, then we will hold onto what we have. YHVH will do what He has to do in the middle of it all to bring systemic change within the way we operate, particularly with finances.

I do not believe that everyone is going to walk into the full measure of what YHVH has in store in the Melchizedek order. Although it is available to everyone, there is a price to pay for walking in it, and it is not easy. Once we get through the process of learning this truth, and begin to develop our character and connection with YHVH, it will change everything.

The process that YHVH takes us through is to bring us to a point of being able to blueprint what is in Heaven on earth. The blueprint that Melchizedek has for financial systems, when they are fully revealed, will completely turn the current financial system upside down. An influencing factor in all our financial dealings is that YHVH will only fit Himself into what looks like Himself. If we go about looking at Babylon and the way it is set up, we will not realise that YHVH's Kingdom has its own financial system. If we are not careful we can miss the reflection of what the Lord desires. This reflection resembles the development of a mountain all on its own. It governs in the right way with the right flow and attitude, with the right things in place. When we start to operate in some of these arenas, the face of the marketplace will change because we will be building our own mountain that has nothing to do with Babylon. The mountains around us will have the appearance of the reflection of YHVH. That is why people will want to be in them. What happened with Solomon when all the kings of the earth came to trade with him, is what will begin to take place with us. We need to build our own power base with its own culture, language, priorities, administration and way that it functions. It is not a downhill function. Rather, it is like a funnel going up. It starts with the small end of the funnel as a birthing chamber on the earth for the overflow of the magnitude of the capacity of Heaven coming down through it. It then builds up until the base of the mountain is at the top, allowing it to contain more and more resources. Where it comes down here will be the birthing chamber that sits here. It is all circular. The mountain is not about people, it is about a movement of a Kingdom to invert the current governmental structure which has a single person at the top with everyone controlling others. It is inverting the current governmental structure to one where everyone is serving one another rather than trying to control others.

For a long time, all of this just sat inside of my heart from hours and hours of sitting with YHVH, looking at creation and doing what I call creative thinking. I have so much caught in my head. Eventually, it comes out in teaching. For me, the release and opening up of the gates of Zion is the key. We must establish seats in the courts of Zion in order to administrate properly. Most people would not even understand what we are talking about. But to be able to sit in that gate and administrate what is coming out of Zion into creation is all about Kingdom business. It is all about the financial arena and the governmental system that is going to begin to govern the earth. It is all about establishing a new government, but not the type of government we know with a president. It is an internal, governmental system that humanity will respond to, not because it has to, but because it wants to. The fruit is going to be there.

Down to Business is part of the process of getting introductory information to people. No doubt as things go on in the future, we will get down to more of the nitty-gritty detail of how we are to operate as we learn how to develop it and mature. It is all a learning process.

CHAPTER 11

WISDOM IN BUSINESS

I have found the purposeful pursuit of building a relationship with the being called the Spirit of Wisdom to be extremely helpful within the business environment. I have already written in chapter seven about her direct involvement within the business arena. Building a relationship with the Spirit of Wisdom does not negate or replace your responsibility and your union with YHVH and the maintenance of this relationship as He is the source.

People have said to me, "How do I build? How do I even start this?" YHVH is always the centrepiece and beginning point of any relationship. He introduces me to those who would be in my immediate sphere of relationships. Once introductions are made, it is up to me to build the personal connection. Flowing on from such a connection and the building of that relationship, I have found that introductions to others come through this new relationship.

If you run a business and you have not built a relationship with the Spirit of Wisdom, then you will primarily have success out of your own hands. YHVH will bless the work of your hands, as the Word says, "...*the LORD your God will bless you in all your work and in everything you put your hand to*" (Deuteronomy 15:10 NIV), but that blessing will be based on what you have done out of the need for your own affirmation. Our goal with regard to business life can be to find affirmation and fulfilment coming through our work. Emotional fulfilment and affirmation are great because of the sense of accomplishment they bring. But if the accomplishment is at the detriment of your relational connection with the Godhead, then your affirmation comes out of your business, not out of your relationship with YHVH. If your affirmation comes from YHVH, then you will find that He will not only bless the works of your hands, but He will bless you as a person and help you grow into levels of maturity and responsibility that will go beyond the earth.

The whole of the celestial arena, the heavens and the universe, really is our Father's business, not just the little businesses that we are doing here. Some of the work we do here in this life trains and prepares us for something that is greater. Therefore, our responses in the middle of this training are really important. If we cannot take care of what is going on here, then it is going to be very difficult for us to have responsibility when we are dealing with galaxies. Part of our problem in business life, and one of the reasons we get so busy in it, is because our identity and our fulfillment comes from trying to achieve something, instead of from our relationship.

I have no issue with working eight to ten hours a day. But if that work comes at the detriment of relationship, particularly within one's family and in one's relationship with YHVH, then for me, there is an immediate problem. It goes back to this question: where does your affirmation come from? For me, it is about building a relationship with the Spirit of Wisdom in the function and relationships of that business. An overflow of wisdom into your business is vital. In reality, this is an outworking of what YHVH wants within creation.

Building relationship with the Spirit of Wisdom has four components. It has your intent, desire, faith and hope. These four things all express themselves and are found and fulfilled in love. They are all connected to the way your heart functions within creation as a being, and in the way that we operate and move in what YHVH wants us to do.

Relationship First

I never go into relationships with the motive of getting what I want. Unfortunately, many of us are like that in our relationship with YHVH.

Every day I would get up between four and six o'clock in the morning, with whatever was in my heart to do, and I would spend that time praying and making my requests known to YHVH. I would tell Him things that I wanted and I would engage with what I wanted to see unfold. I would do that until I realised I had gone beyond making my requests known to YHVH, to making continual demands. It got to the point where it was the only way I thought when I prayed. It dawned on me that I had become a nagging, demanding child and lacked maturity in relationship. There were times when He would do what I asked, which was great. But I found when I repeatedly asked for the same things, He would begin to ignore me. This to me is typical of a church-age, driven mentality toward prayer. Prayer is not a place of demanding, but a place of building relationship where your requests become mutually known through that relationship.

I have found that it is far easier to build relationship and friendship with YHVH if I spend my time building our relationship through connection, friendship and union with Him without my requests. Also, my requests are granted a lot easier than they were through the struggle of making demands because I have built a relationship. My requests are granted because they came out of connectivity; the other way of praying was focused on my needs. If we function out of need, and have not pursued connectivity, then our needs may be met, but we will not have an overflow. I also find this true in business. If my needs are being met through my business but there is not an overflow, it is because I am not engaging with YHVH in relationship.

When I set my heart to engage with the Spirit of Wisdom in business, it is not to merely have her flow through me in the decisions I make. While that flow is a fruit of the relationship connection I build with her, I want the Spirit of Wisdom to have an active involvement and connection to all I am doing. I could see what YHVH was doing through her with what I was given to do within business life. It comes out of relationship, not out of demanding.

If I came up to a friend or an acquaintance one day and said to them, "Hey, I really need ten thousand dollars to do this project. Can you give it to me?" If they were only an acquaintance, I could not expect to receive the money from them. They would probably reply something like, "Get a life: who are you?". However, if I have a good relational friendship and strong connection with them, and I ask the same thing, the result might be different. In return, if they asked the same thing of me and I did not have a relationship with them, my response would be the same. But if they were a close friend, I would move what I could to get the money to them. As a friend, I would have a far more open-hearted response to giving them what they needed than to give to someone who was only an acquaintance.[17]

---

[17] See Marios Ellinas' *Tables and Platforms*, available from Son of Thunder Publications, anticipated Summer 2019 release.

Build Connectional, Not Task-Oriented Relationships

I grew up in the church culture and system. It came with expectations to accomplish tasks. These expectations framed up task-oriented relationships in my life. I had to break this and learn a new process undoing what I had learned in order to relearn how to build proper relationships. Do not only form a task-oriented relationship with the Spirit of Wisdom, so that she is just involved in the things that you are doing. Task-oriented relationships break when the tasks are done.

You have to continually keep your eyes on building relationship. If we build relationship and a task comes up, then together we can do the task. Marriage provides a good example. In it, you have relational connection and fulfillment which comes from the approach "Together, we are labouring to see this happen," instead of "We are labouring to see this happen together." These are completely different statements. The relational connection, through intent, is to engage with the Spirit of Wisdom. Do not have it based around your desire to connect to get what she can give. Build the relationship first, then discuss those things with her and see how she responds within relationship.

Honour Relationship through Process and Peace

The next process that is helpful is relational connection through honour. When the Spirit of Wisdom is engaging with you, particularly in the beginning of the relationship, I have found that she will not entrust you with everything that your heart is thinking about and desiring all at once. When she releases something to you, do not try to work and figure out what she has given you. Rather, allow its natural development, like a seed that takes time to steadily grow. Honour the small things. Actively engage with them and wait for the development of understanding.

I have learned to honour the peace that I have received from her to help me in what I am doing. Out of honouring the peace that I have received, honour opens up the way for more information to come about what was given. This unlocks our understanding to another degree. Again, when I receive something like this, I do not try and figure it all out. I do not sit there trying to plan and map out this small piece of information. I hold it, and engage with it out of honour and with a thankful heart for the measure that I have been given. I know that it will produce fruit: but I also know that if I hold it in honour, it can be enlarged and produce far more fruit.

I found that by going through this process over and over, I very slowly learned how the Spirit of Wisdom functions in relationship, particularly in regard to business.

The Role of Desire

I engage with desire inside of my life. But I do not make all my desires known with my mouth. I engage in relationship allowing my intent to direct where my desire goes. Let's say I have a desire, for example, to have a billion dollars (due to my own personal immaturity). To be able to handle this, I allow time for me to grow through stages of development until I am at a point where resources are released. I will not continue to push, demanding witty inventions that will bring the billion dollars. Behaving that way makes you like a petulant, demanding child who wants something way beyond its maturity. The key is relational maturity.

If there is no ability in you to handle the responsibility of the outworking of the billion dollars, then it will not be released to you. Even if it was given to them, most people would not be able to administrate ten million dollars. It takes many hours to administrate ten million dollars in the right way. I am not talking about business investment when a piece of investment is two hundred million dollars, I am talking about the day-to-day administration of the ten million dollars. A lot of planning that has to go into this process, especially to handle it with integrity and not frivolously. Of course, desire unlocks faith and faith unlocks hope, but the whole thing is based around love. If we do not have love for what we are doing and who we are connecting with, then why are we doing it? When you only have task-oriented relational connections with the Spirit of Wisdom or with Prudence in your daily business life, the expression of relational connection is not valued. Love is not task-oriented: love is relation-oriented. Love is the only thing that is going to remain.

I say to business people, particularly within the household of faith, building relational connection with the Spirit of Wisdom is vital. It is interesting that unbelievers can connect to the spirit world and hear from other spirits that can give earthly wisdom. These are generally called familiar spirits using the ways and the patterns of the people, both alive and dead.

How is this going to be actually worked out in our daily life? One of the key components of engaging the Spirit of Wisdom is to allow her to direct my path. I do this by holding a relational connection in my heart, recognising that she rejoices in my successes. This is not just a spiritual process but also relational. Our spirituality must be ground out into daily life and bring change to reveal the nature of YHVH here on the earth, otherwise it is just spirituality with no meaning. For me, I have to see the reflection of what YHVH is doing in our natural life. He has to be revealed and our spirit life has to be grounded down here in our daily life to where daily life begins to be a reflection of what is truly going on in your relationship with YHVH - Heaven on earth.

Wisdom as the Doorway to Prudence

Proverbs 8 says this, *"I, wisdom, dwell with prudence, And find out knowledge and discretion"* (Proverbs 8:12 NKJV).

One of the components for finding relationship and connection with the Spirit of Wisdom is to unlock the relational connection with the being called Prudence. Some people say Prudence is an angel; I am not so sure of that. I know she is a sentient being who is present with the Spirit of Wisdom. I have found that sometimes people try to engage with Prudence outside of a relational connection with the Spirit of Wisdom. The Spirit of Wisdom is the key component of your doorway of access to the being called Prudence. Without connection to the Spirit of Wisdom, engaging with Prudence is using a back door through the tree of the knowledge of good and evil, and doing so will often result in deception. Do not pursue receipt of something when you have not first pursued relationship. This is not the way you develop connection.

I look at the Kingdom as a many-layered structure. When you go through the right door, it gives you access to those layers. Relationship with Father, Son and Holy Spirit does not automatically give you access to everything else, although you have the right to it. It is all relational.

For example, I will not walk into Melchizedek's treasure chamber and demand riches without walking through the relational protocol with him because he is the door keeper. The Spirit of Wisdom operates in the same way: she is the door keeper to Prudence because Prudence is with her. Once I have built relationship with Prudence, then witty inventions may become the norm. All of life works like this – we need to build relationship before we can have the full benefit of what the other may contribute.

Connecting with the Spirit of Wisdom unlocks the doorway to connect with Prudence, the being that gives witty inventions to men. Receiving witty inventions is not just about getting good ideas, it is actually coming to a point where processes can be advanced so that they become second nature, and often a different way of doing something can be uncovered. Prudence wants to give us witty inventions for real life, not just for greater ideas. Great ideas are awesome. Prudence will very slowly become involved in your normal life as you engage with her. Again, the issue of relationship is so important; we must purposely never make demands on Prudence for witty inventions.

Ten years ago, when I first uncovered who she was and started engaging with her, I realised that I had not built relationship with Prudence. So, it's the same issue: if you build a task-oriented relationship with Prudence, you may be blessed. But if you build a relationship, when you ask you may be given something that goes way beyond what the task you wanted could have ever achieved inside your life.

I want as many witty inventions within my business arena as I can have, flowing on a continuous basis. Witty inventions are not just new ideas, or business ideas, although they can be. They can also teach us how to work and be smarter to overcome obstacles around us and create the capacity in us to be seen from the outside as successful. That of course, becomes a reflection of YHVH, as long as your heart is connected and functioning in the right way. If it is not, then it will create problems for you in your business life.

Business Evidence of a Relationship with Wisdom

What kind of things will be displayed around me when the Spirit of Wisdom is involved? What should my business look like when the Spirit of Wisdom is involved in it? How does it function, what happens with it?

Overflow of Blessings

King Solomon is the scriptural example of what it looks like when the Spirit of Wisdom is involved and immersed in your daily life. All of the kings came and bought offerings to Solomon: "They brought tribute and served Solomon all the days of his life" (1 Kings 4:21 NKJV). Solomon did not need their offerings, but this was physical evidence of the involvement with the Spirit of Wisdom through his life, influencing Israel. The next evidence was peace around all Israel's borders.

The impact of the realm of peace surrounding our business and all that we do is a vital component in Kingdom business life.

The next evidence will be that all of your employees are being blessed. All those who are connected to what you are doing will receive an overflow of blessing from what is coming to your house. You may be the connection point for it, and the faucet it comes through, but all those who are connected to and woven into what you are doing will all begin to be blessed by what YHVH is doing.

One thing I really love about The Nest is that we have been able to take some of what we have received and pass it on. We have been able to bring other people into positions of responsibility and take some of the blessing that is on us and put it on them. This is what the Kingdom is all about. It is not about being selfish with everything that comes in: it is about understanding that there is a flow and YHVH wants this flow to continue. The way the flow continues is through blessing others with an increase. The greater the level of increase we have, the greater the level of increase we can engage with others' lives around us to bring them to the point where there is a corporate display of something that is different than that which is going on out in the world at the moment.

This was evident with all of Solomon's servants. The scripture says that all Solomon's servants were happy (1 Kings 10:8). The word happy can mean overflowing with joy or peacefully content. It is the shalom of the Lord: nothing missing, nothing broken.

The kings connected with Solomon because they saw the effect Solomon had on those around him. Because of this they wanted to have connection to Solomon. One way relationship was built in those days was by bringing gifts and large portions [18]to honour the position of the person one was seeking en-

---

[18] These were portions of anything they had, including gold, silver, spices, oils, animals, servants, soldiers and anything else they had to give as a sign of the value they placed in the one they were giving the gift to.

gagement with. This offering opened a doorway to build a relationship. Giving the offering did not oblige the recipient to extend relationship because the gift was given without strings attached, but it could open a door to build relationship.

In some traditional teachings, Solomon is said to have had people around him all of the time learning from him. They were not only listening to what he was saying to others, but learning about handling and processing things from his business acumen. The governors who provided for his table learned the shortcuts that YHVH had given to Solomon. "And these governors, each man in his month, provided food for King Solomon and for all who came to King Solomon's table. *"There was no lack in their supply"* (1 Kings 4:27 NKJV).

Connections Come to You

The first outworking of connection with the Spirit of Wisdom is people wanting to get connected with what is being revealed because they see the blessing of YHVH sitting on what is happening through what you are doing. Because of their connection to what is going on, there is an outworking of the grace sitting on the environment that helps unlock this process in their lives, and helps accelerate them into their portion. It is about building many mountains of supply, not just building one big fat mountain that everyone has to keep coming back to.

Being around David had a similar effect on his mighty men. I believe they gave into the building of the temple in a massive way from their own personal coffers. They built their own supply through the knowledge of being around David and engaging process in relationship with him. They were knitted to him relationally because of something in him that made it easier for them to flow into what they would then produce. They were overflowing with the blessings of YHVH in their lives. One of the key benefits of building connected relationships is the overflow from one to another that becomes evidence of YHVH's blessing.

"And when the Queen of Sheba heard of the fame of Solomon concerning the name of the Lord, she came to prove him with hard questions" (1 Kings 10:1 KJV).

The next thing that will be revealed, is that others will begin to hear what YHVH is doing within the house of your occupation. Whatever you are doing, whether it is in ministry, business, or other, people will begin to hear of your fame through others. It is amazing to me that I live in New Zealand, but we have people around the world engaging with everything we have been doing. It is almost like it has built a whole new city of things. I do not even know what to call it. It is not a movement. It is a new wellspring of expression of the Kingdom. It is "the people of the way" finding a way to reveal the way here in creation. It is about making YHVH's name famous.

People come and they get connected, because others have testified about the goodness of the Lord in the land of the living (Psalm 27:13). It is not you going to other people saying, "God has been good to me. I have done this and that." It is about others testifying about YHVH's portion around your life.

Solomon did not have to promote himself. People heard through others what was going on and came to see for themselves. He was busy with his own nation and was so occupied with YHVH that he did not have time for the opinions of other people and what they thought about him. His own nation was being blessed by YHVH, which was his prime concern. This was the culmination of the Age of Peace. In the Age of Peace, Solomon expressed what we are going to see in the dispensation to come. No one wanted to make war with Solomon because of the evidence of the blessing around him and his nation.

So engage with YHVH. Stop worrying about what everybody else is doing and do what the Lord is asking you to do. Put your head down and work on what YHVH has asked you to do. Allow YHVH to make you famous. Stop trying to make yourself famous with opinions. You do not have to make yourself famous. If you have what it takes in your relationship with YHVH, YHVH will make it known openly for others to see without you having to do a thing about it. He wants an overflow of blessing to sit around you that it will make a sound of its own so that other people will turn to the evidence of that sound to engage with it.

The desire of YHVH is not to have everything looking exactly the same, but being an individual expression of government to be able to express the diversity of YHVH Himself. It is not about all looking the same, it is about all of us individually revealing the blueprint of what YHVH is wanting in creation. It is not all of us doing the same blueprint. Not every nation could do the same thing that Solomon was doing; but by being connected to Him, there was an overflow that gave them abundance.

Supernatural Answers and Manifest Fruit

> *"And Solomon told her all her questions: there was not anything hid from the king, which he told her not."* (1 Kings 10:3 KJV)

One of the things I have found about engaging relationship with the Spirit of Wisdom is that we will be able to have answers for things that we do not even understand. I have found when someone comes with a hard question, having the answer is fascinating when you are listening to yourself speak. It is like the answer was already in you. You can answer questions they have inside their heart that they did not even ask. When you are engaging in a heart-to-heart with other people, and Wisdom is reflected in what you are doing, she is displayed towards other people around you. Imagine being in a board meeting where people are discussing something, and you come in with a simple word that changes everything going on within that meeting. To me, this is how Solomon operated when he was in discussion regarding his corporate engagement within his nation. I know this because the Word says,

"And when the queen of Sheba had seen all Solomon's wisdom, and the house that he had built, and the meat of his table, and the sitting of his servants, and the attendance of his ministers, and their apparel, and his cupbearers, and his ascent by which he went up unto the house of the LORD; there was no more spirit in her." (1 Kings 10:5 KJV)

We've reviewed this passage earlier, but let's just break down a little bit more here the evidence of connection to the Spirit of Wisdom. The queen of Sheba had seen Solomon's wisdom and the house he built, and here, she is left speechless (see chapter seven). When it says she saw *"...the house that he had built, and the meat of his table..."*, this part of the verse means the overflow of abundance was evidenced in every aspect of provision that was necessary for the functioning of the portion YHVH had given to Solomon in his life. There was evidence of the fruit. There was tangible, real evidence of what was going on around him, because there was abundance.

So, one of the evidences of engagement with the Spirit of Wisdom in business is that you do not have to boast about what you have built. Others will see the evidence in the fruit displayed around you. The fruit will speak for itself. It does not have to be justified nor does it have to be approved. Good fruit will be around you when the Spirit of Wisdom is operating in your life. Not only for you, but there will be abundance of fruit for others to come and begin to glean from what is on your life.

The Spirit of Wisdom is evidenced by visual engagement of a spiritual realm manifesting in the physical realm down here. I find it frustrating when I hear people talking about "wealth transference" who have no visual fruit of responsibility for wealth in their own life. It is great to believe for something for the future, but reality must be the measure of the outworking of what you believe in this life. This means that fruit must be seen where your desire and your intent is focused. It cannot just be hyper-spiritualised. Stop trying to be spiritual and allow the fruit to show. What is the fruit that has been revealed inside of your life as evidence of what you believe?

When the queen of Sheba came into Solomon's temple, she could not recognise who Solomon was, because everyone was dressed in such kingly garments and in such array. Solomon was not seated in a higher seat than anyone else; he was seated on the same level. The only place where he was seated higher than anyone else was when he ascended up into the throne of YHVH's presence. He was seated with all his servants and everyone around him had the same apparel (1 Kings 10:4–5 KJV). Everyone who was directly connected to Solomon had such an overflow of abundance and such pleasure of willingly serving that nothing was done by constraint.

Are the people who are under your overflow coming to a point where what YHVH has blessed you with is resting on them to such an extent that they do not feel isolated from you? Do they see themselves as a part of the blessing of what YHVH is doing within your environment? The ministers around Solomon were all of those who were in charge of areas of responsibility. Their work was not done through constraint or legal requirement or demand. It was done out of relational connection.

Our lifestyle has got to be a reflection of another Kingdom, not of the kingdoms of this world, the seven mountains of this world that are so corrupt. We have to build. Solomon did not build seven mountains and occupy seven mountains that another had built. Solomon built his own mountains, and out of establishing his own mountains, he was able to display a Kingdom from Heaven on the earth. That, to me, is our whole job in what we do in business life. It is to show that realm operating here in every facet: in relationship, connectivity, overflow, abundance, fruit, government, authority and in finances.

I know that YHVH wants to bring influencers. Influencers do not come because one day they decided to be an influencer. A true influencer is someone who goes through training with YHVH themselves, and their character gets developed to a point where they do not need people to affirm them. All they need is YHVH to say, "Well done!"

ABOUT IAN

Ian Clayton is the founder of Son of Thunder Ministries. He passionately pursues a life of understanding and getting to know who the person of God really is.Ian travels itinerantly by invitation throughout New Zealand, Africa, America, Europe and Asia ministering, teaching, equipping and mandating people to become sons of God.

Ian's heart in founding Son of Thunder is to have an avenue to put strategies and keys into believers' hands to enable them to actively participate in the reality of the realms of God's Kingdom and to experience the empowerment of life as the spirit beings we were created to be.

Ian trains and equips believers to give their lives in a persistent, passionate pursuit of the person of God, enabling them to discover that their lives are about the preparation for oneness and unity with God for the purpose of becoming mandated and authorised ambassadors of His Kingdom. His passion is to reveal to the sons of God the purpose of the power of the attorney of God within them, removing the sense of powerlessness and hopelessness that is often attached to many in the body of Christ when they are confronted with the reality of the spirit world that surrounds them.

Find out more at Ian's website, sonofthunder.org.

Down to Business is published by

sonofthunderpublications.org